THE INDISPENSABLE GUIDE
to practically
EVERYTHING

Jesus

THE INDISPENSABLE GUIDE

to practically

EVERYTHING

Jesus

ALTON GANSKY

Guideposts

New York, New York

The Indispensable Guide to Practically Everything: Jesus

ISBN: 978-0-8249-4774-3

Published by Guideposts
16 East 34th Street
New York, New York 10016
www.Guideposts.com

Distributed by Ideals Publications, a division of Guideposts
2636 Elm Hill Pike, Suite 120
Nashville, Tennessee 37214

Guideposts and *Ideals* are registered trademarks of Guideposts.

Acknowledgments
Every attempt has been made to credit the sources of copyrighted material used in this book. If any such acknowledgment has been inadvertently omitted or miscredited, receipt of such information would be appreciated.

Scripture quotations marked CEV are from the Contemporary English Version, copyright © 1995 by the American Bible Society. Used by permission.

Scripture quotations marked MSG are from *The Message*. Copyright © 1993, 1994, 1995, 1996, 2000, 2001, 2002. Used by permission of NavPress Publishing Group.

Scripture quotations marked NASB are from the New American Standard Bible®, copyright © 1960, 1962, 1963, 1968, 1971, 1973, 1975, 1977, 1995 by The Lockman Foundation. Used by permission.

Scripture quotations marked NIV are from the Holy Bible, New International Version®. Copyright © 1973, 1978, 1984, International Bible Society. Used by permission of Zondervan Publishing House. All rights reserved.

Scripture quotations marked NKJV are taken from the New King James Version. Copyright © 1982 by Thomas Nelson, Inc. Used by permission. All rights reserved.

Scripture quotations marked NLT are from the *Holy Bible*, New Living Translation, copyright © 1996, 2004. Used by permission of Tyndale House Publishers, Inc., Wheaton, IL 60189. All rights reserved.

Scripture quotations marked NRSV are from the New Revised Standard Version of the Bible, copyright © 1989 by the Division of Christian Education of the National Council of the Churches of Christ in the United States of America. Used by permission. All rights reserved

Library of Congress Cataloging-in-Publication Data

Gansky, Alton.
  Jesus / Alton Gansky.
    p. cm. – (The indispensable guide to practically everything)
  ISBN 978-0-8249-4774-3
  1. Jesus Christ–Person and offices. I. Title.
  BT203.G36 2009
  232–dc22
                                2009010194

Editor: Lila Empson
Cover and interior design: Whisner Design Group
Typesetting: Educational Publishing Concepts

Printed and bound in the United States of America

10 9 8 7 6 5 4 3 2 1

His is easily the dominant figure in history. . . .
A historian without any theological bias whatever
should find that he simply cannot portray the progress of
humanity honestly without giving a foremost place to
a penniless teacher from Nazareth.

H. G. Wells

Contents

What Was Jesus Like? 69

How Jesus Worked... 103

The World's Greatest Teacher 149

Friends and Enemies 181

The End of the Beginning 203

How Jesus Changed the World 235

Jesus Christ is the same yesterday and today and forever.

Hebrews 13:8 NIV

Introduction

Christ was not a deified man, neither was he a humanized God. He was perfectly God and at the same time perfectly man.

C. H. Spurgeon

It is hard to imagine someone who has never heard of Jesus. He is a global entity. But recognizing Jesus' name and knowing about him are different things. Jesus is the best-known person in history. He lived two millennia ago, and yet people are still discussing him. For some he is a historical character; for others he is a good teacher; others consider him a prophet; and hundreds of millions of Christians call him Lord.

This is amazing considering he lived in a time with no mass communication, slow transportation, and only word of mouth to get word out. Yet, he is the founder of a church that operates in nearly every country of the world.

More books have been written about Jesus than about any other person. He has been the subject

We look at this Son and see the God who cannot be seen. We look at this Son and see God's original purpose in everything created. For everything, absolutely everything, above and below, visible and invisible, rank after rank after rank of angels—everything got started in him and finds its purpose in him. He was there before any of it came into existence and holds it all together right up to this moment.

Colossians 1:15–17 MSG

of plays, novels, nonfiction books, movies, articles, sermons, and more. People dedicate their lives to him and work in careers that are rooted in his teaching.

This book is an effort to help people know a little more about Jesus. It is designed to be an indispensable guide to Jesus. That's not to say what follows is a complete work of Jesus' life. It is not. Personal bookshelves hold scores of books dealing with Jesus. If all the pages were counted, they would number in the tens of thousands—maybe more.

Still, the book has value. An attempt has been made to touch on the key elements about Jesus and his work. Some of the topics that follow deserve books of their own. This book can be read bit by bit and referred to in the future. The specialized language of the theologians has been done away with. This is a look at Jesus in simple, straightforward language.

Bible verses are drawn from several major English translations. Each chapter ends with a set of questions to keep the mental juices flowing. It is hoped this book opens doors of thought for you and becomes a handy reference.

Our mind is where our pleasure is, our heart is where our treasure is, our love is where our life is, but all these, our pleasure, treasure, and life, are reposed in Jesus Christ.

Thomas Adams

God exalted him to the highest place and gave him the name that is above every name, that at the name of Jesus every knee should bow, in heaven and on earth and under the earth, and every tongue confess that Jesus Christ is Lord, to the glory of God the Father.

Philippians 2:9–11 NIV

"Come, see a Man who told me all things that I ever did.
Could this be the Christ?" Then they went out of
the city and came to Him.

John 4:29–30 NKJV

Discovering Jesus in the Pages of the Bible

The New Testament is a compilation of books that reveal Jesus and his times. It is through the four Gospels that we learn the most about Jesus.

Contents

There are also many other things which
Jesus did, which if they were written in detail,
I suppose that even the world itself would not
contain the books that would be written.

John 21:25 NASB

How the Bible Reveals Jesus

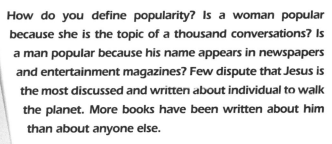

How do you define popularity? Is a woman popular because she is the topic of a thousand conversations? Is a man popular because his name appears in newspapers and entertainment magazines? Few dispute that Jesus is the most discussed and written about individual to walk the planet. More books have been written about him than about anyone else.

The events surrounding Jesus took place two thousand years ago, at a time when there were no reporters, no news cameras, no documentary filmmakers to record his words and deeds. So how do we know what we know?

Almost every home in America has at least one Bible. Some have a dozen. For some, Bible reading is a daily activity; others never touch the book. Every year approximately 175,000 new books are published. This happens year after year, and yet no other book has eclipsed the Bible in importance or scope.

Despite its appearance, the Bible is not really a book—it is a library. The Protestant Bible contains 66 individual books, written by 40 different authors, on three continents, over a period of 1,500 years. The authors used three languages: Hebrew, Aramaic, and Greek. There are 31,173 verses divided into 1,189 chapters totaling 774,746 words

Jesus provided far more God-revealing signs than are written down in this book. These are written down so you will believe that Jesus is the Messiah, the Son of God, and in the act of believing, have real and eternal life in the way he personally revealed it.

John 20:30–31 MSG

We proclaim to you what we have seen and heard, so that you also may have fellowship with us. And our fellowship is with the Father and with his Son, Jesus Christ.

1 John 1:3 NIV

(the equivalent of nearly 10 novels). If all we knew about the Bible were limited to those statistics, we might think the Bible to be a mishmash of contradictions, but it isn't. Over the centuries, the Bible has shown itself to be accurate in everything it speaks about.

To the Christian mind, everything in the Bible points to Jesus. From the first book, Genesis, to the last book, Revelation. The ancient scholar and Bible translator Jerome put it this way: "Ignorance of the Scriptures is ignorance of Christ."

The earliest reference to Jesus is found in the Bible's first book. "He shall bruise you on the head, and you shall bruise him on the heel" (Genesis 3:15 NASB). Bible scholars have dubbed these few words the *protoevangelion* ("first gospel"). This short verse is a promise from God that a solution to the sin in the garden of Eden would be dealt with by a special person. That person was Jesus.

There are approximately four hundred references to Jesus in the Old Testament. (The Old Testament is the part of the Bible that deals with history up to the time of Jesus. The New Testament covers the life of Jesus and years following his ministry.) A reader can find references or allusions to Jesus in every book of the Bible. These references come in a variety of forms, from specific prophecies and direct mentions to more subtle foreshadowing.

The old saying "Hindsight is 20/20" has bearing here. We stand two millennia from the days Jesus walked the earth. We're even further away from the earliest Bible writers who penned their portions of Scripture fifteen hundred years before Jesus. But standing where we do gives us an advantage. We can look back with greater insight. Old Testament passages do not reference Jesus by name but by his nature and actions. In fact, those four hundred or so references can be applied to only one person. Jesus alone fits the bill.

Fifteen hundred years ago, Saint Augustine said about the Old and New Testaments, "The New is in the Old contained; the Old is in the New explained." The two parts of the Bible are hand and glove, each incomplete without the other.

In the Old Testament we see Jesus as active in creation (Genesis 1:26; compare to Colossians 1:16); as the promised Messiah (Isaiah 7:14); as dying on the cross (Psalm 22; Isaiah 53); as humanity's redeemer (Job 19:25); as rising from the tomb (Psalm 16:10); and more.

> You have been taught the holy Scriptures from childhood, and they have given you the wisdom to receive the salvation that comes by trusting in Christ Jesus.
>
> 2 Timothy 3:15 NLT

The entire New Testament centers on Jesus and the church he founded. The first four books, called the Gospels, are biographical accounts of Jesus and his ministry. The book of Acts shows Jesus' ascension and the growth of the church. The Epistles (*epistle* refers to a letter sent from writer to reader) provided guidance to the various churches based on Jesus' life and teaching. The book of Revelation shows future events leading to Jesus' second coming.

Although several ancient documents refer to Jesus, the Bible is our most complete source of information about him.

Theologian David S. Dockery said, "This overarching unity centers in Jesus Christ, who is the primary subject and key to interpretation of Holy Scripture." Through eyewitness testimony, the Bible paints the picture of Jesus in great and historic detail.

Something to Ponder

The Bible has many parts: personal accounts, poetry, histories, letters from the apostles to the church, and more. Despite its many literary styles of multiple authors, writers who lived in very different times and under various circumstances, the Bible remains a single unit with a single message: The world needs a savior, and Jesus is the only one who fits the bill.

The Bible is our telescope and microscope to the person, nature, teaching, and works of Jesus Christ. Without it, we would know very little about Jesus. With it, we have more than we can possibly learn.

Final Thought

 The pages of the Bible serve as our time machine. Its record of God's work through his Son, Jesus, takes us on a journey of understanding—a journey that changes forever. All it takes to begin is to open the book and start with the New Testament Gospels.

Check Your Understanding

- **The Bible is a library of how many books?**

The Protestant Bible has sixty-six books—thirty-nine Old Testament books and twenty-seven New Testament books.

- **Although the Bible was written by many writers, it has one primary subject. What is that subject?**

The Bible covers many topics, but at its heart is a single individual: Jesus.

- **The Bible has two major sections. What are those two sections?**

The Old Testament and the New Testament. The first section begins with creation and continues until a few centuries before Jesus. The second section covers the life of Jesus and the early church.

What Makes the Gospels So Great?

Everything we know about Jesus comes from four New Testament books: the Gospels. *Gospel* means "good news." In the pages of these four books, we learn of Jesus' birth, miracles, ministry, enemies, sacrifice, death, burial, resurrection, and ascension. We see how he interacted with others, how he taught, what he taught, the love he showed, the strength he exhibited, and much more.

Four men undertook the task of writing down much of what Jesus did. We cannot discuss *all* that he did. It would be difficult to sum up everything in a single book. Still, what we have is amazing and inspiring.

Every writer wants a best seller, to have his books read everywhere. Today a best seller might be read by tens of thousands, and a top best seller might sell a few million copies. At some point, however, sales fall and the book goes out of print.

Four men—Matthew, Mark, Luke, and John—wrote short books that are read around the world and have been for two thousand years. What keeps readers coming back? The subject: Jesus, a subject they knew very well.

The Gospel writers were apostles or had an apostle associated with the work. The word *apostle* refers to someone sent on a mission. Jesus' closest followers were later called apostles because they took the message of Jesus to the world.

> It seemed good to me also, having had perfect understanding of all things from the very first, to write to you an orderly account, most excellent Theophilus, that you may know the certainty of those things in which you were instructed.
>
> Luke 1:3–4 NKJV
>
> This is the good news about Jesus Christ, the Son of God.
>
> Mark 1:1 CEV

Matthew was one of Jesus' disciples and wrote from the point of view of an eyewitness. He wrote what he saw. The same was true for John. Mark and Luke had a different approach. Mark, who wrote the earliest Gospel, was not one of the twelve disciples. Most scholars agree with the tradition that states Mark's Gospel is really Peter's Gospel. Mark put the ink on the page, but he did so under the guidance of the apostle Peter. There are scores of clues in the book that point to Peter.

Luke, like Mark, was not one of the original disciples. He was a physician who became a believer and undertook a detailed research project to learn and compile a record of the life and work of Jesus. The result is the Gospel of Luke.

Points to Remember

Each Gospel has a unique point of view. Matthew and John wrote from three years of personal experience with Jesus. Mark told the story from the apostle Peter's perspective, and Luke wrote his Gospel after extensive interviews and research. The result is a cohesive and vivid account of Jesus' life.

Check Your Understanding

- **What does the word *gospel* mean? Why is it important?**

Gospel *means "good news." It refers to the message of Jesus' life and sacrifice.*

- **There are four Gospels. What makes them different from one another?**

Perspective. Each Gospel emphasizes different aspects of Jesus' life. It's more than one person's point of view. The first three are similar in taking the same approach to the story of Jesus and are often called the Synoptic Gospels. Synoptic *means "to see together." John's Gospel is very different.*

Why We Can Trust the Gospels

"Almost our only sources of information about the personality of Jesus are derived from the four Gospels, all of which were certainly in existence a few decades after his death. He is a man. This part of the tale could not be invented."

The above quote comes from H. G. Wells, author of eighty books and many shorter works. Although not necessarily friendly to Christian teaching, he did recognize the reliability of the Gospels. If we hope to understand Jesus, we must have a reliable source of information. The four Gospels provide an accurate portrayal of Jesus and his life.

Our world has taught us to be skeptics. In a time when we are bombarded with hundreds of marketing messages a day, it pays to be a bit of a skeptic. Life calls upon us to pass judgment on every bit of e-mail we receive, every circular that shows up in our mailboxes, and every commercial that comes over the radio or television. We size up the people we meet: *Are they trustworthy? Should I be careful around them? Are they telling me the truth?*

It's natural for some to be skeptical about the accounts in the Gospels. After all, they contain some difficult-to-believe events: walking on water; raising the dead, performing miraculous cures, multiplying food meant for one person to feed thousands, and doing scores more trust-stretching acts. For some it is easier simply to deny the accounts than to believe they occurred.

Faith comes from hearing the message, and the message is heard through the word of Christ. But I ask: Did they not hear? Of course they did: "Their voice has gone out into all the earth, their words to the ends of the world."

Romans 10:17–18 NIV

So many others have tried their hand at putting together a story of the wonderful harvest of Scripture and history that took place among us.

Luke 1:1 MSG

Yet they cannot be ignored. Day after day they touch lives, bring comfort, and most of all reveal the unique person named Jesus. Can we trust those four books of the New Testament? The answer is yes, and here are a few reasons why.

First, we need to know that although the books are two thousand years old, there is no doubt about their authenticity. There exist more than five thousand manuscripts or pieces of manuscripts available for study. (This is true for much of the New Testament.) Scholars have compared these documents to one another and discovered that they are nearly identical in the stories they record and the ways in which they tell them. Why are there so many manuscripts? Because the early Christians had a hunger to know about Jesus. The Gospels were copied by hand repeatedly.

There is more evidence for the reliability of the Gospels than for any other ancient document. For example, there are only twenty copies of *Annals*, a text written by Tacitus around the same time the Gospel books were being written. And the oldest extant copy of *Annals* was penned a thousand years from the date the original was written. Similar things can be said about Caesar's *Gallic War* (only ten copies available); Pliny the Younger's *History* (seven manuscripts); and Aristotle (at most five copies of any single work). When you read a contemporary translation of the Gospels, you can do so knowing that the weight of thousands of manuscripts has guaranteed you have an accurate rendering of what was written in the first century.

The character of the writers plays an important role in the veracity of the Gospels. Tradition tells us that John was the only disciple to die a natural death; the rest were martyred in one hideous fashion or another. By writing the Gospels, they put their lives on the line even more. The early church was brutally persecuted. Writing the life of Jesus made them larger targets.

The writers also included material that embarrassed them or made them look foolish. Events such as Peter's denial, Thomas's doubt, and the bickering over who would be first in the kingdom of God are not the kinds of things most writers would record about themselves.

The Gospels are historically accurate. They mention names like Herod and Pilate; places like Jerusalem, Bethlehem, and many others; events like the census that forced Mary and Joseph to travel to Bethlehem, and much more. These names, places, and events have been verified many times over.

This disciple is the one who told all of this. He wrote it, and we know he is telling the truth.

John 21:24 CEV

Other writers near the time when the Gospels were written and being spread throughout the known world quoted from the books without hesitation.

If the Gospels are accurate and truthful about persons, places, and events, that can be easily verified. Doesn't it make sense to think they are accurate about the other events they record?

A great deal of research has shown time and again that the Gospels are trustworthy and to be believed. They provide a clear view of Jesus, a view we can trust and believe in.

Something to Ponder

Mark Twain quipped, "It ain't those parts of the Bible that I can't understand that bother me, it is the parts that I *do* understand." The critics of the Gospels often fall into this camp. Let's face it: the message of Jesus is demanding on the believer. It requires facing ourselves with a new light, and that can be uncomfortable. Truth is often that way.

To believe the accounts in the Gospels means believing in a need for forgiveness, a need for a Savior's sacrifice, a belief in miracles, and a belief that God works in our lives today.

Final Thought

Who believes the Gospel accounts? The educated and those with little education; executives and laborers; teachers and students; engineers and scientists; craftsmen and artists; young and old; and people from every nationality and country. People from every area of life have learned that the Gospels are trustworthy.

Check Your Understanding

- **How does the character of the Gospel writers help us trust their writing?**

Considering the cost the writers paid to be Christians during the persecution helps us understand how committed they were to the truth. If they didn't believe what they wrote, then it would make no sense to endure such hardship.

- **How does the historical accuracy of the Gospels prove the books to be reliable?**

If the Gospels contained many inaccuracies about people, places, and events, then it would open the doors of doubt about the rest of their material.

- **Why does it matter that there are so many manuscripts available for the Gospels?**

Having more than five thousand manuscripts, pieces of manuscripts, quotations in other works, etc., enables scholars to compare writings and demonstrate that the Gospels we have today are the same as those written two thousand years ago.

Gospel Differences

Once, it was popular among the wealthy to have their portraits painted. It doesn't take an art scholar's eye to see that portraits of the same individual differ from one another when painted by different artists. These differences come about because no two artists see things the same. The Gospels are portraits, with each author an artist committed to emphasizing some aspect of Jesus. Matthew, Mark, Luke, and John set out to portray Jesus and did so with great accuracy and skill. The Gospels were not meant to be identical. Just the opposite. They were meant to emphasize different facets of Jesus' life.

✳

Each Gospel writer set out to achieve a specific goal and emphasized what he thought would be the most instructive for his readers. Let's have a look at those differences.

The book of Matthew shows Jesus as a King. The ancient Jews expected a Messiah who would lead them to political and spiritual freedom. Jesus is that Messiah. Matthew's account highlights Jesus' teaching and contains more of his sermons than any other Gospel. Matthew relied heavily on the Old Testament, directly quoting or alluding to approximately 125 passages. *Matthew wanted us to hear Jesus.*

We have the word of the prophets made more certain, and you will do well to pay attention to it, as to a light shining in a dark place, until the day dawns and the morning star rises in your hearts. Above all, you must understand that no prophecy of Scripture came about by the prophet's own interpretation. For prophecy never had its origin in the will of man, but men spoke from God as they were carried along by the Holy Spirit.

2 Peter 1:19–21 NIV

The book of Mark, however, shows Jesus as a suffering servant. Mark is the shortest of the Gospels and probably the first one written. Mark emphasizes Jesus' actions, recording eighteen miracles but only four parables. Much of the Gospel focuses on the Passion Week—the eight days from Jesus' entry into Jerusalem to the resurrection. *Mark wanted us to watch Jesus.*

Luke shows Jesus as the perfect Man and lays out the universal appeal of Jesus' message, often referring to sinners and outcasts. Luke is fact-based and shows more history about Jesus and his work. Luke emphasized the personal side of the gospel. *Luke wanted us to see the personal Jesus.*

John's Gospel is unique, emphasizing Jesus as God's divine Son. John did things differently. For example, he didn't mention Jesus' birth or lineage but did show the preexistent Jesus at creation. *John wanted us to see the divinity of Jesus.*

Myth Buster

Some state that the Bible is filled with contradictions. These people often point to the Gospels, saying parallel accounts contain variations. These are not contradictions. Each Gospel writer set out to paint a portrait of Jesus that highlighted certain aspects of his nature and work and stressed a particular lesson.

Check Your Understanding

- **Do we really need four Gospels? Wouldn't one larger Gospel have been better?**

Having four Gospels is an advantage. One longer Gospel would not allow us to experience the many layers of Jesus and his teaching. In this case, more is better.

- **What is the advantage of seeing an account from different perspectives?**

Different perspectives allow us to see Jesus from different points of view. The writers present a unified story but with different insights, and the variations let us see the many facets of the gospel message.

The Men Who Wrote the Gospels

The Bible is both a supernatural and a human book. Human authors wrote under inspiration a book that has never been matched. No other work carries the deep insight, the moral teaching, and the obvious fingerprint of the divine. Often called the Word of God, the Bible came to be through human writers, each with a history, and each with a story of his own. Matthew, Mark, Luke, and John are household names. Known for their association with Jesus and the early church, they should also be remembered as the most read writers in history. Just who were these men?

Matthew, also called Levi, was a tax collector. No one likes to see the tax collector coming, but in Jesus' day, the stigma was far worse. People loathed tax collectors, not because they took hard-earned money from the citizens but because they turned most of the money over to Rome. A Jew collecting taxes from other Jews to give to an oppressive, occupying nation like Rome was considered the lowest work a man could do. Tax collectors made their money by adding a surplus to the tax. That was Matthew's place in society: despised, avoided, his only friends other tax collectors.

Passing along, Jesus saw a man at his work collecting taxes. His name was Matthew. Jesus said, "Come along with me." Matthew stood up and followed him.

Matthew 9:9 MSG

Only Luke is with me. Get Mark and bring him with you, for he is useful in my ministry.

2 Timothy 4:11–12 NRSV

Matthew 9:9 tells how Jesus saw Matthew sitting in the tax collector's booth, approached him, and uttered two words, "Follow Me" (NKJV). Matthew did. He became one of the twelve men chosen to follow Jesus. An interesting tidbit: Matthew mentioned coins more often than did any other Gospel writer, something natural for a former tax collector.

Mark is most likely John Mark (again a man with two names). In the Gospels, we learn that he lived with his mother, Mary. It appears that Mary was a woman of some wealth and owned a home large enough for Jesus and the disciples to celebrate the Last Supper. Other meetings were held there (Acts 12:12). When the mob came to arrest Jesus, a young man followed, and many think that man was Mark. The arrest came late at night. In his haste to see what happened to Jesus, the young man covered himself with a linen sheet. He was nearly captured.

Mark would join Paul and his cousin Barnabas on a missionary trip but leave before it was over. He eventually would go on other mission trips. Sometime later he became associated with Peter. The apostle called him "my son" (1 Peter 5:13). It was during this time that Mark wrote his Gospel under the direction of Peter.

Luke wrote two New Testament books: the Gospel of Luke and the book of Acts. The Gospel of Luke covers the life and ministry of Jesus; Acts reveals events of the early church. In Acts Luke recounted the missionary journeys of Paul. In some of those accounts he switched from third person (Paul sailed to . . .) to first person (We sailed to . . .), indicating Luke accompanied Paul on some of the trips.

Called the "beloved physician" (Colossians 4:14), Luke gave some of the most detailed accounts of Jesus' activities. His writing style shows that he was an educated man. He was the academic of the Gospel writers.

John not only wrote the Gospel of John but also three epistles (letters) and the book of Revelation, a record of a vision he received while exiled on the island of Patmos. He and his older brother James (as well as several other disciples) were fishermen and worked for their father, Zebedee. John was an insightful man who expressed himself in simple terms. He wrote in the simplest Greek, and his Christian motto was, "Children, love one another."

He was also a man of courage. After Jesus' arrest, he was the only disciple willing to follow him to the cross. John was one of the first to hear of Jesus' resurrection, and he and Peter were the first to examine the empty tomb.

Although John wrote simply, his writing is profound. His Gospel stands apart from the others in tone, content, and approach. He, Peter, and James made up the "inner circle" of the disciples, the closest of the close. He never referred to himself by name in his Gospel, but did call himself "the disciple whom Jesus loved" (21:7 NIV).

> Peter and John answered, "Do you think God wants us to obey you or to obey him? We cannot keep quiet about what we have seen and heard."
>
> Acts 4:19–20 CEV

Of all the disciples, only John died a natural death. All the others died while continuing the ministry of Jesus. That isn't to say John had it easy. He suffered under persecution and was exiled, but nonetheless he outlived all his friends and companions.

Something to Ponder

The four Gospels are accounts written by men who couldn't be more different: Matthew, a tax collector; Mark, a travel companion to Barnabas, Paul, and later Peter; Luke, a physician moved to write a comprehensive biography of Jesus; and John, a plainspoken fisherman. Two, Matthew and John, were part of the chosen 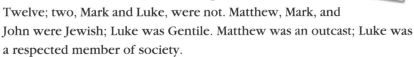 Twelve; two, Mark and Luke, were not. Matthew, Mark, and John were Jewish; Luke was Gentile. Matthew was an outcast; Luke was a respected member of society.

The backgrounds of the Gospel writers show how the message of Jesus cuts across social lines, education, and personal history. It is open to everyone.

Final Thought

 What can be said about the Gospels can be said about the entire Bible: It was written by real people to real people to help us live godly lives in a real world. It is all there for the reading.

Check Your Understanding

- **Does it matter that the Gospels were written by common men instead of by religious or political leaders?**

There is no doubt God inspired men from different walks of life and different experiences to pen the Gospels. It is easier to relate to people who have been through similar or greater trials.

- **Does the particular background of one of the Gospel writers appeal to you more than the others?**

Each Gospel emphasizes different aspects of Jesus and his ministry. One Gospel may resonate with us more, but all were written for our benefit. The story of Jesus' life is incomplete without all four Gospels.

- **Why do you suppose the writers went through the trouble of producing the Gospels?**

For them and all Christians, the story of Jesus is the most important story ever told. Not to share it would be a crime.

The Land and People of Jesus' Day

The land and time Jesus lived in would strike most of us as unusual and unsettling. It was a difficult period filled with hard work and uncertainty. Yet Jesus was not born into that land by mistake; it was part of God's plan. To understand Jesus' ministry, we need to know a little about the land and people of his day. These people followed him, came to him for help, and listened to his sermons. Some were the people who would challenge him, mock him, and ultimately hang him on a cross.

✳

Most people were farmers, herdsmen, or craftsmen. They worked hard and received by our standards very little for it. Wealth was confined to a few landowners. The rest of the people lived in simple, one-room mud homes, working the fields or crafts during the day.

Everything revolved around family, worship, and work. The Jews instilled their beliefs into everything, taking great pains to rear children who knew the Mosaic laws. However, even religion provided oppression. Many religious laws made life difficult, and several powerful sects competed for influence over the masses.

Many people spoke up to three languages: Aramaic (a language similar to Hebrew) served as the daily language; Greek was the business language; and because of the Roman presence, Latin was spoken.

He was chosen before the creation of the world, but was revealed in these last times for your sake. Through him you believe in God, who raised him from the dead and glorified him, and so your faith and hope are in God.

1 Peter 1:20–21 NIV

When the people saw the sign that he had done, they began to say, "This is indeed the prophet who is to come into the world."

John 6:14 NRSV

Rome ruled with a heavy hand, levied steep taxes, and did things offensive to first-century Jews, such as controlling activities at the temple.

Uprisings were common. Groups were formed for the express purpose of killing Romans. Pontius Pilate, who would be governor during Jesus' ministry, hated Jews, and Jews returned the sentiment. History records an event in which Pilate ordered the slaughter of a group of Samaritans.

Still, Rome did bring roads, security, and law to the land, but at a price. The hatred would reach the boiling point in AD 70 when Rome destroyed the temple and much of Jerusalem, killing tens of thousands.

As difficult a time and land as it was, Jesus operated his ministry there, and he forever changed the world.

Take It to Heart

We do not choose where we are born. In free countries, we make changes in our lives and improve our situations. Jesus did something different. He sought no wealth, no improvement of his condition. Instead, he chose to improve the lives of others by offering a spiritual strength found only in him.

Check Your Understanding

- **Why do you suppose God chose such a unique time in history for Jesus' arrival?**

It was the perfect place and time. Rome made travel easy with its extensive roads; Greek provided a common language. The people were ready for a Messiah to teach them what God truly wants.

- **Do you think Jesus' ministry would have spread faster if he had been wealthy?**

No. The people then, as now, needed a Savior they could relate to. Jesus was one of them. Like many, he would suffer at the hands of the Romans.

Jesus' Arrival

At Christmas, people around the world celebrate the arrival of Jesus and have done so for two thousand years. The way he arrived teaches us a great deal about him.

Contents

She will bear a son, and you are to name him Jesus,
for he will save his people from their sins.

Matthew 1:21 NRSV

Jesus Before His Birth

It is a difficult concept for many to grasp, but Jesus existed before his birth. Sounds odd, but it is nonetheless true. When Christians speak of the preexistence of Jesus, they mean that he existed in the eternal past. In short, there was never a time when Jesus was not. The Bible holds many passages about Jesus before his birth, and Jesus himself claimed an eternal existence. The life of Jesus does not begin with his birth; he has no beginning.

Theologian Herschel Hobbs said, "The story of the life of Jesus Christ did not begin in Nazareth or Bethlehem but in eternity. It is true that Jesus of Nazareth was God; it is even more correct to say that God became Jesus of Nazareth."

The preexistence of Jesus is one of the most important doctrines. The deity of Jesus rests on it. The virgin birth is unique in history, but it is not what made Jesus the Savior. His teaching, healing, and sacrifice make sense only if he was truly God incarnate.

One thing that makes the Gospel of John distinctive is how he began his work. He did not start with the birth of Jesus, as did Matthew and Luke. He began before time. John 1:1 reads, "In the beginning was the Word, and the Word was with God, and the Word was God" (NKJV).

By him all things were created: things in heaven and on earth, visible and invisible, whether thrones or powers or rulers or authorities; all things were created by him and for him. He is before all things, and in him all things hold together.

Colossians 1:16–17 NIV

The Bread of God came down out of heaven and is giving life to the world.

John 6:33 MSG

It is almost impossible to understand, but God took on flesh. John said it this way: "The Word became flesh and dwelt among us, and we beheld His glory, the glory as of the only begotten of the Father, full of grace and truth" (John 1:14 NKJV).

Many passages show Jesus as Creator. Jesus claimed preexistence: "I didn't come from heaven to do what I want! I came to do what the Father wants me to do. He sent me" (John 6:38 CEV). If we trust him in other things, we must also trust him in this.

Final Thought

Although he was God in the flesh, he was every bit human. He felt cold and heat; he hungered and thirsted; he needed sleep; he felt pain; he laughed and wept. Jesus left behind greater things than can be found on this earth, but he found us worth it.

Check Your Understanding

- **Does it really matter that Jesus has existed eternally?**

Yes. His preexistence is evidence of his deity, authority, and qualification to be Lord and Savior.

- **Does it matter that we don't fully understand how Jesus can be God in the flesh?**

No. We have sufficient information, but we will probably never fully understand. Some things are beyond human comprehension. Most of us do not understand the details of how electricity is generated, transmitted to our homes, and made available with the flip of a switch, but still we do not hesitate to turn on the lights.

What He Left Behind to Come Here

The new pastor had left a beautiful small town near the ocean to take a church in the desert. One of the parishioners, while on vacation, traveled through the pastor's former community. When he returned he approached the minister after church and described how he had traveled to where the pastor had lived. He paused and then asked, "Are you crazy? Why would you leave that place for the desert?" We might be forgiven for harboring the same thought when considering what Jesus left behind to come to earth.

✳

Jesus' leaving heaven is like a painter becoming a brushstroke on his painting, or a playwright becoming a character in his own play. For some it is easier to imagine putting all the oceans in a teacup or trapping the atmosphere in a bottle than it is to understand that God would take on human form and walk this planet.

Jesus left behind many things to visit this world. First, he left the glory of heaven. We know very little about what heaven looks like. We know it is inhabited by God, his angels, and believers who have died. Revelation describes it as a beautiful place (21:1–22:7). Trying to describe it properly is beyond human language.

By coming to earth as a human, Jesus took on certain limitations

Think of yourselves the way Christ Jesus thought of himself. He had equal status with God but didn't think so much of himself that he had to cling to the advantages of that status no matter what. Not at all. When the time came, he set aside the privileges of deity and took on the status of a slave, became human! Having become human, he stayed human. It was an incredibly humbling process. He didn't claim special privileges. Instead, he lived a selfless, obedient life and then died a selfless, obedient death— and the worst kind of death at that—a crucifixion.

Philippians 2:5–8 MSG

and weaknesses. For example, the timeless One became bound by time, by the passing of day and night. Formerly, he was above time, unaffected by its passing. On earth time ticked by for him as it does for all of us.

God is described as being omnipresent—present everywhere at all times (Psalm 139:7-12). There is no place in heaven or on earth a person can go where God is not. During his earthly ministry, Jesus was bound by our three spatial dimensions.

He also took on basic human needs for food, rest, warmth, shelter, and more. In heaven he had no such needs, but on earth he felt hunger and thirst, weariness, and emotional and physical pain.

Take It to Heart

Christ uncrowned himself," William Dyer wrote, "to crown us, and put off his robes to put on our rags." Jesus made great sacrifices for us. He left behind glorious things so he could take us in. There is much to admire about our planet; there is much to look forward to in heaven.

Check Your Understanding

- When we think of Jesus' sacrifices we usually think of the cross, but he made many others. What do those sacrifices teach us?

His sacrifices show the strength of his love for humanity. The highest sacrifice is the cross, but we shouldn't overlook all that he left behind.

- If someone said, "Love isn't defined by what we give, but by what we give up," would you agree?

There is certainly some truth in that. Love is expressed in the giving of ourselves, but it is also demonstrated by what we're willing to give up for someone else.

An Angelic Birth Announcement

There is good news, bad news, and stunning news. Mary, the mother of Jesus, received the latter one day in Nazareth. Until that moment, Mary was just another young woman living in a small town and thinking about her pending marriage. Her life was filled with the same day-to-day work that occupied the lives of other women. Then something she couldn't imagine happened, something that would make her the most famous woman in history. Today her name brings to mind the qualities of obedience, strength, courage, and commitment.

Only the Gospel of Luke records the announcement of Mary's pending virgin birth (Luke 1:26–38). Luke, the Gospel writer who went to great lengths to interview and research the life of Jesus, gave us the details. It is very likely that he learned these details from Mary herself.

The angel Gabriel was sent by God to deliver a one-of-a-kind message to a young woman in the small town of Nazareth. Gabriel is unique among the angels. We know of only three angels by name: Gabriel, Michael the Archangel, and Lucifer, a fallen angel. Gabriel's name means "hero of God," and he appeared to three individuals in the Bible. First, he was sent to the Old Testament prophet Daniel to explain visions he had seen. He was not heard from again until he appeared to Zechariah, John the Baptist's father (Luke 1:5–25). In his conversation with the priest, Gabriel said, "I am Gabriel, who stands in the presence of God,

I will tell of the decree of the LORD: He said to me, "You are my son; today I have begotten you. Ask of me, and I will make the nations your heritage, and the ends of the earth your possession."

Psalm 2:7–8 NRSV

Watch for this: A girl who is presently a virgin will get pregnant. She'll bear a son and name him Immanuel (God-With-Us).

Isaiah 7:14 MSG

and I have been sent to speak to you and to bring you this good news" (Luke 1:19 NASB).

On the other side of the conversation was Mary, a young woman many think may have still been in her teenage years. We can't be certain of her age, but it was not uncommon for a woman in her late teens to be part of an arranged marriage. We know very little about Mary.

How Gabriel appeared to Mary is not revealed. Other places in the Bible show angels popping in, but here we are not told. "Greetings, favored one! The Lord is with you" (Luke 1:28 NASB). Mary was puzzled by the greeting. "Favored one" indicates a person given a place of great honor. Mary must have wondered what honor that was.

Gabriel told her not to be afraid. When angels appear to humans, these are often their first words. Apparently, the appearance of an angel is

frightening. He then made the big announcement: "Don't be afraid! God is pleased with you, and you will have a son. His name will be Jesus" (Luke 1:30-31 CEV). Again, Gabriel told her she had found favor with God. Something about Mary made her special to God and qualified for a unique honor: bearing God's Son. Before she could come to grips with that statement, she learned that she, a virgin, would bear a son. Not just a child, but a son. She must have wondered how Gabriel could know the gender. He also told her the child's name.

Gabriel then made a power-pact statement. This child would (1) be great; (2) be called the Son of the Most High (God); (3) be a king in the lineage of David; (4) reign over his people forever; and (5) have no end to his kingdom. Mary would have recognized all the terms indicating Jesus would be the Messiah.

Of course, Mary was confused. She was a virgin, and virgins do not deliver babies. Naturally, she asked how this could be. Gabriel had an answer: "The Holy Spirit will come down to you, and God's power will come over you. So your child will be called the holy Son of God" (Luke 1:35 CEV). It is impossible to say with certainty exactly what all that entails, but the wording and result suggest a creative act. As God made the universe from nothing, he would create his Son within Mary.

Perhaps the most amazing part of the story was Mary's response to Gabriel: "I am the Lord's servant! Let it happen as you have said" (Luke 1:38 CEV). It is difficult to imagine the courage it took to say those words. She agreed to have her life changed forever.

Digging Deeper

It is doubtful that Mary understood exactly why she was chosen and how God would work in her body the miracle Gabriel announced, but she was willing to move forward. Mary would have understood Gabriel's meaning. Every Jew looked forward to the day when the Messiah would arrive. Of all the women in the world, she had been chosen for the honor. She was to be the mother of the Messiah, the mother of the "Son of the Most High." From that moment on, her life would be different.

Final Thought

Gabriel brought an astonishing announcement, one that would forever change Mary's life and would have far-reaching effects on her family and her husband-to-be. Yet she recognized the importance of what was happening to her and made herself available to God's will. Her courage was amazing.

Check Your Understanding

- **Did anything in Mary's background prepare her for such a high calling?**

Since we know so little about her family and background, it's difficult to say. As a Jewish woman, she looked forward to the coming of the Messiah. To hear she was to be part of the process must have been as thrilling as it was terrifying.

- **Why does the Bible mention Gabriel by name?**

The few times we hear of Gabriel, he has been sent with a history-changing message. This was the most important message he could announce.

- **In reading the biblical account, do you get a sense of Gabriel's emotional state?**

He seems proud and joyful to be bringing the message.

- **Today we have a detailed understanding of human reproduction, something not true in Mary's day. Still, she knew how a woman became pregnant. What do you suppose her first thought was?**

Impossible. Mary knew she was a virgin, and she knew it took two to make a baby. Gabriel's announcement must have seemed to be nonsense, yet she didn't respond with ridicule but with acceptance.

- **Mary asked how such a thing could be, and the answer the angel gave didn't explain everything. But she accepted the news as fact. Why?**

Most likely because of the messenger. If anyone other than an angel had brought such news, her response might have been different.

- **Do you suppose Mary understood the details and what it would all mean?**

Doubtful. Her submission is one of the greatest examples of faith found in the Bible.

Can the Virgin Birth Be Real?

In December 1903, the Wright brothers were successful in getting their "flying machine" off the ground. Thrilled, they telegraphed this message to their sister Katherine: "We have actually flown 120 feet. Will be home for Christmas." Katherine hurried to the editor of the local newspaper and showed him the message. He glanced at it and said, "How nice. The boys will be home for Christmas." He missed the importance of the event. That same editor, if told the young Mary was miraculously with child, might say, "How nice. She's going to have a baby." Jesus arrived by miracle.

No subject surrounding Jesus is as controversial as the virgin birth. It goes against everything we know about human reproduction. Only a miracle can explain what happened.

The angel Gabriel appeared to Mary to deliver a message that is remembered every Christmas (Luke 1:26–38). Mary is unique among all women and favored of God. She was to be the mother of the Savior of humankind.

Then came the shocker: "You will conceive in your womb and bear a son" (Luke 1:31 NASB). Despite her youth, she certainly understood how children came to be. She also knew she was a virgin. If the statement had been made by anyone other than an angel, he would have been laughed out of town. Gabriel not only announced her pending pregnancy but stated the child would be a boy. Something no one could know.

Coming in, he said to her, "Greetings, favored one! The Lord is with you."

Luke 1:28 NASB

When the time arrived that was set by God the Father, God sent his Son, born among us of a woman, born under the conditions of the law so that he might redeem those of us who have been kidnapped by the law. Thus we have been set free to experience our rightful heritage. You can tell for sure that you are now fully adopted as his own children.

Galatians 4:4–6 MSG

Why a virgin? Wouldn't Jesus be Jesus if his conception had been typical? No. The virgin birth achieves several things. First is Jesus' sonship. Jesus is the Son of God. He is the second person of the trinity. He is God in the flesh. The virgin birth dispels doubt about Jesus' parentage. No man could claim to be his father.

It also reminds us that our salvation is supernatural, that is, "above nature." God did what no man could do. This makes Jesus unique. His physical birth made our spiritual births possible.

Myth Buster

 At times, someone will suggest that Mary's virgin pregnancy is only a rare human example of parthenogenesis. Parthenogenesis is a form of asexual reproduction that happens naturally in some sharks and reptiles. It has never been observed in humans, but even if it were to be, the offspring would be a female.

Check Your Understanding

- **What difference would it make if Jesus' birth had been like every other human birth?**

The key here is to understand that Jesus' unique birth made him unique among all humanity and shows the divine nature of Jesus. Without the virgin birth, it might be argued that Jesus was just a good man.

- **Why do you suppose so many deny the virgin birth?**

The virgin birth is hard to believe. It goes against what we know. That, however, doesn't make it any less real. Miracles are events that surpass nature.

Mary the Mother

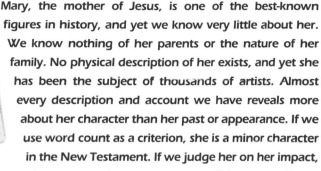

Mary, the mother of Jesus, is one of the best-known figures in history, and yet we know very little about her. We know nothing of her parents or the nature of her family. No physical description of her exists, and yet she has been the subject of thousands of artists. Almost every description and account we have reveals more about her character than her past or appearance. If we use word count as a criterion, she is a minor character in the New Testament. If we judge her on her impact, she numbers among the greatest personalities ever to live.

She lived in Nazareth, a town so insignificant it's not mentioned anywhere apart from the New Testament. No one would have looked at Mary and said, "That girl is going to make history."

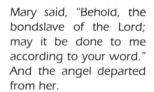

Mary is mentioned only twenty-three times in the New Testament, and sixteen of those mentions deal with the birth of Jesus. Her parents are never mentioned, causing some scholars to assume she was an orphan. Apocryphal literature suggests that Ann and Joachim were Mary's parents.

Mary faced the most difficult situations imaginable. An angel appeared and announced she was to be the

> Mary said, "Behold, the bondslave of the Lord; may it be done to me according to your word." And the angel departed from her.
>
> Luke 1:38 NASB
>
> Mary treasured up all these things and pondered them in her heart.
>
> Luke 2:19 NIV

mother of the Messiah, the Son of God. The book of Matthew tells us she was betrothed to a man named Joseph. If this betrothal followed the custom of the day, then Joseph was considerably older than Mary. In Mary's day, engagement was as binding as marriage. To become pregnant during the betrothal would forever shame Mary, Joseph, and their respective families.

Mary showed no reluctance to be the "servant of the Lord." We can only imagine what she endured during her pregnancy. Had Joseph not been encouraged in a dream to take Mary as his wife, he would have broken the engagement, rendering her unloved and unwanted.

Mary's response revealed inspiring character traits. Despite the unheard-of proclamation, she remained unshaken. She asked questions revealing a keen mind. The biblical text says she pondered (Luke 1:29) these things, a habit revealed during other key events in her life. Her contribution is immeasurable.

Final Thought

 When faced with the impossible, she believed; when faced with the difficult, she committed; and when faced with uncertainty, she submitted. Consequently, she deserves credit for her courage, admiration for her acceptance, and praise for her participation in God's plan.

Check Your Understanding

- **Why do you suppose God would choose a young woman from an insignificant town to be the mother of his Son?**

We can't know all the reasons, but we can see Mary's strength, intelligence, and willingness to serve despite the personal cost. Clearly a deeply spiritual woman, she possessed an uncommon inner strength.

- **Do you think Mary understood everything that awaited her?**

No. She would face many difficult times including witnessing Jesus' crucifixion. The same traits that made her a strong and willing servant helped her through the darkest days any mother could experience.

Joseph the "Father"

Often in movies or television shows, there is a character or two that "steal the show." Perhaps they get the best lines, provide a better performance, or just resonate with the viewers. Yet no matter how sensational the performer, he or she needs other actors. These character actors lend depth to the story but are often forgotten once the show is over.

Joseph, Mary's husband, played a pivotal role in the events surrounding Jesus' birth, but he is often overlooked in the Christmas story. This is a shame because he proved himself to be a man of great character.

☧

We know little about Joseph. We know he lived in Nazareth and was betrothed to Mary. Again, betrothal was as binding as marriage, differing only in living arrangements and sexual intimacy. No doubt, he looked forward to his wedding day. Imagine his shock when Mary took him aside and repeated the angel Gabriel's remarks. What man could believe such a story on the first hearing?

He is called a "righteous man" (Matthew 1:19 NKJV). That is high praise. It meant he had deep spiritual roots and members of society looked up to him. Then Mary told him she was a pregnant virgin. Much is made of the ridicule Mary endured. Joseph would have received the same treatment, especially after he decided not to break the betrothal agreement.

 When Jesus began to preach, he was about thirty years old. Everyone thought he was the son of Joseph.

Luke 3:23 CEV

The birth of Jesus took place like this. His mother, Mary, was engaged to be married to Joseph. Before they came to the marriage bed, Joseph discovered she was pregnant. (It was by the Holy Spirit, but he didn't know that.)

Matthew 1:18 MSG

He was a carpenter (Matthew 13:55), a member of an honorable profession. Few structures in that day were made of wood, so carpenters used their skill to fit homes with roofs and to make furniture, wagon wheels, and other items of wood. He passed on the trade to Jesus.

Joseph is mentioned one last time in the story of an event that occurred when Jesus was twelve. He, Mary, and other family members traveled to Jerusalem for a religious feast. Huge crowds descended on the city during those observances. Joseph and the rest of the family left for home, only to find that Jesus was missing. They returned to Jerusalem to find him. Joseph doesn't appear in the Bible again. Most likely he died sometime after the event and before Jesus started his public ministry.

Final Thought

Joseph gets little space in the Gospels, but his role shouldn't be overlooked. He was a man put in a difficult situation. His reputation was at stake and perhaps his business affected, yet he chose the road of spiritual service. In many ways, he exemplifies what a man should be.

Check Your Understanding

- **In Joseph's day, women had few rights. What does it say about Joseph that he would be willing to stay with Mary in such unusual circumstances?**

Although our information about Joseph is limited, what we do know paints a portrait of a courageous man willing to suffer ridicule and damage to his reputation for someone he loves and for his God.

- **Why do you suppose Joseph is so often overlooked when we think of the Christmas story?**

It is an unintentional oversight. Mary and her miraculous pregnancy are so prominent that we fail to see Joseph.

The Day Mary Gave Birth

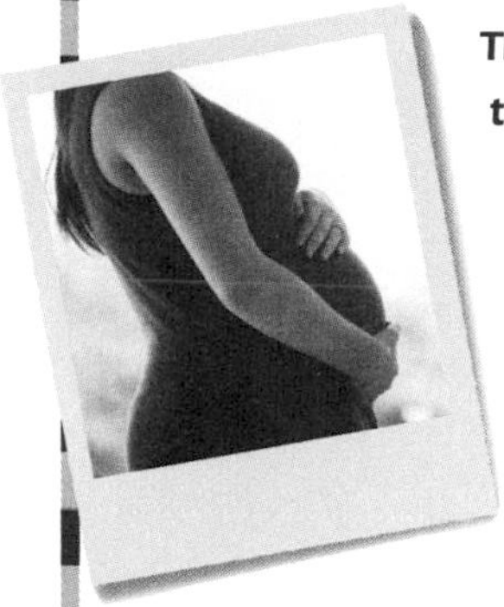

The Christmas story is bittersweet. There is great joy over the birth of Jesus, especially when we understand that he came to redeem us all. Knowing God cares for us that much is heartening. But when properly seen, there is a sense of sadness: a teenage girl pregnant by miracle with only Joseph to believe her, away from home when she went into labor, and forced to deliver in a place never meant for human habitation. Mary was a young woman of rare character. There is no doubt why she was chosen.

The best we can tell, Mary and Joseph were anything but wealthy. Had we been there we might have called them unlucky. They had come to Bethlehem to fulfill an obligation to register for a census. The couple traveled from their home in Galilee to Bethlehem many miles to the south.

Why had she made the trip? First, the time of her delivery was close and Joseph most likely did not want to leave her alone. Perhaps no one there would take her in. Second, they knew the child was to be the long-awaited Messiah, and Bible prophecy foretold that his birth would take place in Bethlehem (Micah 5:2).

Travelers filled the village, and all the possible places to stay were filled. Mary went into labor, and the best shelter they could find was a stable. Did her mind run back through the months to the day Gabriel told her she had been chosen?

> While they were there, the time came for her baby to be born. She gave birth to her first child, a son. She wrapped him snugly in strips of cloth and laid him in a manger, because there was no lodging available for them.
>
> Luke 2:6–7 NLT
>
> You, O Bethlehem of Ephrathah, who are one of the little clans of Judah, from you shall come forth for me one who is to rule in Israel, whose origin is from of old, from ancient days.
>
> Micah 5:2 NRSV

When Mary first saw Jesus, she must have viewed him through tear-filled eyes. In her hands, she held the promised Child, the infant she had carried through the rumors, insults, and cruel laughter. She held God's Son.

Tucked away in the corner of a small village, sequestered in a stable surrounded by the smell and noise of animals, Mary gave birth. She is unique among women, but the process of delivery was the same. She and Joseph were the first to see, to hear, and to touch the Savior. Bethlehem continued on as if nothing had happened.

Take It to Heart

 J. I. Packer observed, "The Christmas message is that there is hope for a ruined humanity—hope of pardon, hope of peace with God, hope of glory—because at the Father's will Jesus Christ became poor, and was born in a stable so that thirty years later he might hang on a cross."

Check Your Understanding

- **What character strengths did Mary show?**

Mary showed submission to God's will, physical and mental strength, determination, and commitment to do right no matter the cost. Like us, she had plans for her life, but those plans were changed and she embraced the change.

- **Given the situation, do you think Mary felt abandoned by God?**

We have no record that she did, and it is doubtful that such feelings occurred. Faith is remaining committed even if life gives us unexpected challenges. The lesson is this: doing right can be emotionally expensive, but the greater good should prevail.

The Little Town of Bethlehem

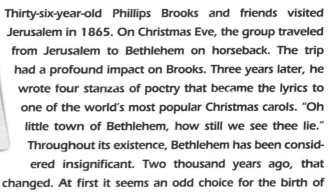

Thirty-six-year-old Phillips Brooks and friends visited Jerusalem in 1865. On Christmas Eve, the group traveled from Jerusalem to Bethlehem on horseback. The trip had a profound impact on Brooks. Three years later, he wrote four stanzas of poetry that became the lyrics to one of the world's most popular Christmas carols. "Oh little town of Bethlehem, how still we see thee lie." Throughout its existence, Bethlehem has been considered insignificant. Two thousand years ago, that changed. At first it seems an odd choice for the birth of Jesus, but there is more to the town than most know.

Bethlehem is a village six miles south of Jerusalem. Nestled in hill country, it lies approximately twenty-five hundred feet above sea level. Through its history, the town has been known by several names: Ephrath, Bethlehem Judah, Bethlehem Ephrathah, and others. *Bethlehem* means "house of bread."

The small city has a long history. References on ancient clay tablets mention the town as early as the fourteenth century BC. King David's ancestors lived there, which is why Joseph was compelled to travel from Nazareth for the census.

Although little noticed in history, Bethlehem was at the forefront of God's plan. Seven hundred years before the event, the place of Jesus' birth was made clear. Micah prophesied, "One will go forth for Me to be ruler in Israel. His goings forth are from long ago, from the days of eternity" (Micah 5:2 NASB).

Does not the Scripture say that the Christ will come from David's family and from Bethlehem, the town where David lived?

John 7:42 NIV

You, Bethlehem, in the land of Judah, are by no means least among the rulers of Judah; for from you shall come a ruler who is to shepherd my people Israel.

Matthew 2:6 NRSV

The portrait of Jesus is painted with symbolism. He was born in a humble town, to humble parents, and in an even more humble situation. Jesus was born according to prophecy and in the town of Israel's most famous king, David. Being in the kingly lineage shows him to be the expected king.

Today when we think of Bethlehem, we think of the birth of Jesus. We see the humble conditions, we note the insignificance of the town, but we also recognize that out of a difficult situation, God's plan took on a personal and physical form in the person of Jesus. Something he did for us.

Take It to Heart

Today, many thousands travel from distant locations to visit the place of Jesus' birth. Jews, Muslims, and Christians consider the town a holy place. However, it is not the place that matters; it is the person born there. In that town, hope arrived for the world and for the ages.

Check Your Understanding

- **There were reasons that Bethlehem was the place of Jesus' birth. What strikes you as important?**

Kings are usually born in palaces in capital cities. Jesus was born in a village no one considered important. Jesus elevated everything he touched including the town in which he was born.

- **The story of Jesus' birth is well known. What is it about his humble birth that is so appealing?**

His humble birth matched his humble life. He could claim rights to all wealth but chose near poverty instead. This makes him approachable, not aloof and distant.

What Is a Manger and Why Is It Important?

Every year thousands of Christmas cards are mailed around the world. Most bear artwork depicting the Christmas story. Many will show an infant in a manger scene. These are beautiful and give us a sense of joy. The place of Jesus' birth is nothing like the sanitized paintings. Instead, he arrived in this world surrounded by the filth of an animal stall. It is odd that the Son of God would be born not in a palace but in a pen meant for animals and laid in a feeding trough. Yet this birth says much about Jesus' love for humanity.

✳

When Queen Elizabeth II visited the United States, she came with four thousand pounds of luggage; two outfits for every occasion; an outfit for mourning (just in case someone died); two valets; a hairdresser; and many attendants. The visit cost about twenty million dollars. As we have seen, Jesus came in poverty, and was naked, delivered in a cave, and laid in a manger.

What is a manger? Ask most people, and they will describe the manger scene, complete with animals, Joseph and Mary, shepherds, and the wise men. The manger, however, is just a single item in that scene. Mangers were stone feeding troughs from which animals would eat. Sometimes these were made from clay mixed with straw or stones and cemented with mud. Many were large rectangular limestone blocks with a trough carved into the top.

A child has been born for us. We have been given a son who will be our ruler. His names will be Wonderful Advisor and Mighty God, Eternal Father and Prince of Peace.

Isaiah 9:6 CEV

If I then, the Lord and the Teacher, washed your feet, you also ought to wash one another's feet. For I gave you an example that you also should do as I did to you.

John 13:14–15 NASB

It's a joyful event set in a sad scene: a man and a woman (and perhaps a hired midwife) sheltered in a cave, sharing the space with animals. After the birth, Jesus was wrapped in strips of cloth and set in the trough.

What does the manger scene mean? It meant God became little. This is difficult to understand. It is easier to believe in a God bigger than the universe than to believe he took on human form.

In *The Jesus I Never Knew,* writer Philip Yancey helps us understand with an illustration from his life. He tells of his experience with his salt-water aquarium. He labored over the tank: vitamins, antibiotics, sulfa drugs, enzymes, water filtered through glass fibers, charcoal, and ultra-violet light. He fed the fish on a meticulous schedule. Yet every time his

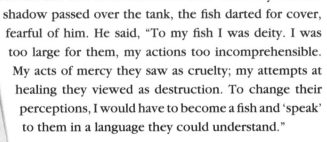

shadow passed over the tank, the fish darted for cover, fearful of him. He said, "To my fish I was deity. I was too large for them, my actions too incomprehensible. My acts of mercy they saw as cruelty; my attempts at healing they viewed as destruction. To change their perceptions, I would have to become a fish and 'speak' to them in a language they could understand."

The Bible speaks of Jesus' deity and refers to him as a King. Yet his first resting place was a trough from which animals ate every day. It was common and lacking anything of the spectacular, yet it shows us the extent to which God will go to express his love.

As is often the case in the Bible, there is a great deal of symbolism in this scene. The birthplace of Jesus foreshadowed his place of death. When Jesus was born, Mary wrapped him in cloth bands as was the custom of the day; when they took Jesus off the cross they prepared his body in the typical Jewish custom of winding bands of cloth around him in a mummylike fashion from his feet to under his arms.

At his birth, Jesus was laid in a manger. In death, he was laid on a stone shelf called a bier. Angels announced his birth; angels attended his resurrection. Mary gave him birth; another Mary—Mary Magdalene—was the first to see him resurrected. The cave was borrowed, as was the tomb. The name *Bethlehem* means "house of bread"; as an adult Jesus would

> You know the grace of our Lord Jesus Christ, that though He was rich, yet for your sakes He became poor, that you through His poverty might become rich.
>
> 2 Corinthians 8:9 NKJV

call himself the "bread of life" (John 6:35 NASB). Jesus was born in a cave in Bethlehem because of a Roman governor's decision to conduct a census; Jesus went to the cross because a different Roman governor condemned him to death.

Jesus came as a commoner so common people could relate to him. No one looked at Jesus and said he lived a privileged life. He was born in difficulty and died in difficulty. Being born as he was makes Jesus approachable.

Something to Ponder

The Jews looked for a conquering Messiah. Rome was a hard taskmaster. Romans hated Jews, and the feeling was mutual. They wanted a mighty Messiah. Instead, Jesus came not as a conquering king, but as a baby in an out-of-the-way town. His arrival was humble and lowly.

This did not happen by accident. Jesus' ministry was foreshadowed by the manger. He would lead a humble life, kept on the outskirts of main-street life. His place would be with the poor and the hurting. He lived and died as he arrived.

Final Thought

Herschel Hobbs wrote, "Thus was the Son of God born. Not in a king's palace nor in the home of the wealthy or mighty, but to a peasant mother whose delivery room was a stable."

Take It to Heart

We look at manger scenes and feel warmth. Mary and Joseph looked at the area in desperation. It was not a choice they wished to make, but one they had to make. It was the last place any woman would choose to deliver her child. The sacrifice Jesus made for us began at birth.

Check Your Understanding

- Do you think all that happened to Joseph and Mary was an accident?

Neither an accident nor coincidence, but everything that happened was all part of God's overall plan.

- Why would God allow his Son to be born in such humble circumstances?

If Jesus had been born in a palace, it would be difficult for many of us to relate to him. Jesus is Savior to all people, rich and poor.

- When we look at an artist's rendering of the manger scene, what should we see?

We should see many things, but most of all we should see the point where God took on flesh and did so for our benefit.

Eyewitnesses: Shepherds, Wise Men, and Angels

The birth of Jesus shook the universe. Does that sound like an exaggeration? True, very few people in Bethlehem, let alone the world, knew what happened, but over time the world would know. Still, there were those who got word early: shepherds, the wise men, and even angels.

The message cut across social classes, touched the poorest, drew the wealthiest, and involved beings of another realm. Why shepherds? Why wise men? Why angels? The answers reveal how universal the gospel is, how all-inclusive its message. Luke 2:8–20 tells the story. The news of Jesus' birth went out with lightning speed.

If we could travel back to that time and tell people angels were going to deliver a message to shepherds, we would have been laughed at. Shepherds sat on the lowest rung of the social ladder. They were considered uncouth, uneducated, uncultured, and illiterate, and they were poorly paid. Few considered shepherds more important than the sheep they tended. Socially despised, economically depressed, and outside the world of religious respectability, they were simple people with simple tasks. No one aspired to be a shepherd.

These men knew only one level of life, then in a minute that changed. An angel appeared and delivered the message (Luke 2:9-14), and what a message it was. It was personal ("born for you" [v. 2 NASB]); it was global ("great joy which will be for all the people" [v. 10 NASB]). It was a detailed message charged with positive

After Jesus was born in Bethlehem village, Judah territory—this was during Herod's kingship—a band of scholars arrived in Jerusalem from the East. They asked around, "Where can we find and pay homage to the newborn King of the Jews? We observed a star in the eastern sky that signaled his birth. We're on pilgrimage to worship him."

Matthew 2:1–2 MSG

words. A baby had been born *to* Mary but born *for* them. This baby was the Savior, the Christ, and the Lord, all terms that meant the long-awaited Messiah had arrived—as a baby. The details continued with the angels telling them they would find a baby in, of all things, a manger.

The outcasts had become insiders. The ignored had become the first to hear of Jesus' birth. Word went not to the powerful, the influential, or the rich. It went to shepherds.

Of course, angels knew what was coming. Gabriel told Mary about her pending miraculous pregnancy. What the angels may not have known was to whom they were to give the message. We might imagine an angel asking God if they should tell the human leaders, only to hear God say, "No. Tell those shepherds."

Angels remain a mystery to us. Although there are approximately three hundred references to these beings, we know very little about them. We do know they are servants of God who act as messengers. In fact, the word *angel* means "messenger." After the angel delivered the message, other angels suddenly joined him, chanting, "Glory to God in the highest, and on earth peace among men with whom He is pleased" (Luke 2:14 NASB).

Angels brought the message, but the shepherds acted on it. They wasted no time walking to Bethlehem and searching for the baby. The text is charged with terms of speed: "go straight," "came in a hurry" (Luke 2:15-16 NASB). Once there, they told Mary and Joseph of the angelic message, something the Bible says Mary treasured and pondered in her heart.

Others would arrive, but not until much later (Matthew 2:1-12). Wise men from the East came to welcome the new King. *King* is the right word. The wise men, also called magi, were the intellectuals of the day, and in their land they were considered kingmakers. These men were not Jews and most likely came from what is now Iraq.

They traveled a great distance, as much as five hundred miles, and when they reached their location they approached the king of the land, Herod, to ask a question certain to upset him: "Where is He who has been born King of the Jews?" (Matthew 2:2 NASB).

> The angel said to them, "Do not be afraid. I bring you good news of great joy that will be for all the people. Today in the town of David a Savior has been born to you; he is Christ the Lord. This will be a sign to you: You will find a baby wrapped in cloths and lying in a manger."
>
> Luke 2:10–12 NIV
>
> Glory to God in the heavenly heights, peace to all men and women on earth who please him.
>
> Luke 2:14 MSG

They found Jesus, not in the manger but in a home with Mary. Then these wealthy, powerful, intellectuals bowed down and worshipped Jesus. They brought gifts of gold, frankincense, and myrrh. Gold was a gift for a king; frankincense was used in religious worship and therefore was a gift for a priest; myrrh was used to embalm the dead and foreshadowed the death of Jesus. Having been warned by God in a dream to avoid King Herod, they returned home by a different route.

God used angels to deliver the first complete gospel message. He used shepherds to prove that the message was for everyone of every class. He used the wise men to show that Jesus' ministry was global, reaching beyond the borders of his land and into Gentile territory. The message of Jesus is meant for every ear and every heart.

Myth Buster

Every Christmas, people put up manger scenes complete with the wise men. Truth is, the wise men were never at the birthplace. We know this because of clues in the text. First, it says they went to a "house," not a stable. Second, the text uses the Greek word for *child* and not *infant*. Later, Herod had all the boys around

Bethlehem two years old or younger killed, implying that it took up to two years for the wise men to arrive. Most scholars believe it took six months to two years to make the journey.

Final Thought

Shepherd or wise man, the gospel has something for everyone. The key is hearing the message and making it part of our daily lives. Jesus came as Savior for everyone, not a select few. He sees no difference between lowly shepherds and lofty wise men.

Check Your Understanding

- **How did the shepherds change after hearing the angelic announcement and visiting the baby Jesus?**

They gained a new view of God, a new view of the future, and a new view of themselves.

- **How do you think the angels felt about the birth of Jesus?**

We can glean from their words that they saw it as a magnificent event.

- **Christmas gift giving began with the wise men. What is the difference between their gift giving and ours?**

They gave gifts to Jesus rather than to one another.

The Amazing People in Jesus' Lineage

Genealogy is a growing hobby. Many of us have an interest in what heroes or villains are in our backgrounds. Tracking down relatives has become an obsession for some. In Jesus' day, lineage was extremely important. For Jesus to be considered King of the Jews, he needed to have the proper genealogy. Matthew and Luke record his significant ancestors for us. Matthew works through Joseph's line, and Luke works through Mary's. Most of us tend to skip over these sections, but they contain some fascinating references.

The genealogies in Matthew and Luke are unique if for no other reason than that they contain the names of four women. Women were not usually included in such lists. To make things even more interesting, the women have "baggage."

Tamar (Genesis 38:6-30) was an Old Testament widow without a child. Children were the only means of support in one's old age. To be without children was often seen as a curse. During those days, the people practiced levirate marriage. The brother of the dead husband was to take his sister-in-law as his wife, to provide for her, and father children for her. Tamar's husband died, and the man who should have taken her in refused. In the end, she seduced her father-in-law. It is also important to know that Tamar was not Jewish; she was an outsider.

> There were fourteen generations from Abraham to David, another fourteen from David to the Babylonian exile, and yet another fourteen from the Babylonian exile to Christ.
>
> Matthew 1:17 MSG
>
> They have those famous ancestors, who were also the ancestors of Jesus Christ. I pray that God, who rules over all, will be praised forever! Amen.
>
> Romans 9:5 CEV

Rahab (Joshua 2:1-24) is an Old Testament hero who risked her life to save two Jewish spies sent into Jericho. When city officials came looking for them, she hid them and misled the search party. She was also a prostitute.

Ruth (Ruth 1–4) lost her husband, brother-in-law, and father-in-law, leaving her alone to manage with just the help of her mother-in-law, Naomi. Ruth is a love story, but what makes her unique in Jesus' lineage is that she was not Jewish.

Bathsheba (2 Samuel 11:1–5) became David's mistress. She was more victim than perpetrator. Before it was over, she would become pregnant, and her husband would be killed to protect David's reputation. The child would later die.

Final Thought

 It would have been easy to leave these women out of Jesus' lineage. Few if any would know, but Matthew and Luke felt they were important. Why? Jesus' ministry is one of inclusion. A person's history does not matter. Jesus equips people to face themselves and their future.

Check Your Understanding

- **How much does it matter that there are flawed characters in Jesus' lineage?**

It means a great deal. While Jesus is perfect, his ancestors were as flawed as the rest of us. To Jesus, the past does not matter but the future does.

- **Each of the four women listed in Jesus' lineage experienced events that made them outcasts. What does that say about God's ability to work in difficult situations?**

Through Jesus, our past can be put in perspective and the future embraced. What we are going to do matters more than what we have done.

King Herod's Horrible Response

The coming of Jesus demands a response. We have seen what the shepherds did, how the angels responded, and the lengths to which the wise men went to bring gifts to Jesus. There is another recorded response, and it's one of the most horrible accounts found in the New Testament. It is all contained in one line: "When Herod realized that he had been outwitted by the Magi, he was furious, and he gave orders to kill all the boys in Bethlehem and its vicinity who were two years old and under, in accordance with the time he had learned from the Magi" (Matthew 2:16 NIV).

The magi visited Herod and asked a question that shocked him: "Where is He who has been born King of the Jews?" (Matthew 2:2 NASB). Herod's first thought must have been, *"I'm the king of the Jews."* His scholars recognized that Bethlehem was the place where the Messiah was to be born, and Herod sent the wise men off, asking them to return with word of what they found. But they didn't. Warned by God in a dream, they took a different path home. Herod lost his mind.

Murder was nothing new to Herod. He had his wife executed. Some years later, he had two of his sons killed because he felt they were a threat to his throne. Later he would have a third son killed. A man who kills his own children will have no reluctance to kill the children of others.

After the scholars were gone, God's angel showed up again in Joseph's dream and commanded, "Get up. Take the child and his mother and flee to Egypt. Stay until further notice. Herod is on the hunt for this child, and wants to kill him." Joseph obeyed. He got up, took the child and his mother under cover of darkness. They were out of town and well on their way by daylight.

Matthew 2:13–14 MSG

Since Bethlehem was only six miles from Jerusalem, it took very little time for Herod's men to carry out the deed. The anguish of the parents was beyond imagination.

Jesus was born into a difficult time and a harsh land. One of the first things he faced was a murder attempt. His life and the lives of Mary and Joseph were spared because an angel warned Joseph in a dream (Matthew 2:13) to flee with his family to Egypt.

The thing about Jesus is that he always brings about a response. Many accept and worship him; others reject him. Herod wanted no changes, but the birth of Jesus brought changes nonetheless.

Final Thought

There is irony here. Jesus did not come to overthrow Herod or any earthly king. He came to deliver a message that would change the world. As God in the flesh, he was already King over far more than Herod's territory. Jesus had a different kingdom in mind—our hearts.

Check Your Understanding

- **As troubling as Herod's actions were, they were not unique. The world is a difficult and unfair place, even for Jesus. What should that tell us?**

One thing it should tell us is that Jesus understands hardship and danger because he has lived through it; therefore, he can understand anything we go through.

- **Herod's greatest fear was that Jesus would change things; would replace him as king. What lesson is there in that understanding?**

When one comes to Jesus, he or she can expect changes, and those changes should never be feared.

What Was Jesus Like?

No man has been studied and scrutinized more than Jesus. No human is quoted more often than Jesus. What was Jesus really like?

Contents

Jesus Christ is the same yesterday and today and forever.

Hebrews 13:8 NIV

Jesus' First Public Appearance

Jesus' first official public appearance happened at the Jordan River. Emerging from the crowds that stood along the banks, Jesus entered the public eye in an unexpected way, by entering the water. The major player was a man known as John the Baptist, Jesus' older cousin. In a quiet act of humility, Jesus launched his ministry. The first three of the Gospels record the account, and John gives a brief description of what happened (Matthew 3:13–17; Mark 1:9–11; Luke 3:21–22; John 1:32–34).

John the Baptist was the forerunner for Jesus. His job was to turn the hearts of the people back to God that they might be receptive to Jesus' message. He was the last Old Testament prophet, rough in appearance and direct. He spent his days preaching about the coming Jesus.

Baptism means "to dip," "to immerse in water." John proclaimed his message, calling the people to repentance. Those who responded were baptized, confessing their sins. His message was always, "After me will come one who is more powerful than I, whose sandals I am not fit to carry" (Matthew 3:11 NIV).

Jesus appeared from the crowd and joined John in the Jordan to be baptized. John felt unqualified and objected, saying he needed to be baptized by Jesus. Jesus insisted and John complied.

Jesus came from Galilee to John at the Jordan, to be baptized by him. John would have prevented him, saying, "I need to be baptized by you, and do you come to me?" But Jesus answered him, "Let it be so now; for it is proper for us in this way to fulfill all righteousness." Then he consented. And when Jesus had been baptized, just as he came up from the water, suddenly the heavens were opened to him and he saw the Spirit of God descending like a dove and alighting on him. And a voice from heaven said, "This is my Son, the Beloved, with whom I am well pleased."

Matthew 3:13–17 NRSV

John immersed Jesus, and when Jesus came up three amazing things happened: First, the heavens were opened. Here the word *heavens* refers to the visible sky as if a doorway between our world and heaven opened. Next, the Holy Spirit descended as a dove would and settled on Jesus. Then came a voice from heaven: "You are My beloved Son, in You I am well-pleased" (Mark 1:11 NASB).

Jesus' first official public appearance was an act of humility. John called people to repent and to show that repentance by baptism. Being sinless, Jesus had no need to repent, and yet he did so to set an example for the rest of us.

Final Thought

While the event was public, it had a very private component. The sky opening, the Spirit descending, and the voice of God coming were experienced by Jesus and John the Baptist only (John 1:32). This is one of several times Jesus, the Holy Spirit, and God are seen in one frame.

Check Your Understanding

- **Why would the Holy Spirit descend like a dove?**

The dove represents meekness, a hallmark of Jesus' ministry. The dove was one of the sacrificial animals used by the poor. The dove reminds us that Jesus will become our sacrifice.

- **If Jesus and John the Baptist were indeed the only two to see the heavens open and hear God's voice, then why did God bother with the display?**

God did this to affirm the beginning of Jesus' ministry, to verify for John that he had done the right thing, and to show God's pleasure.

How Jesus Faced Temptation

Life is filled with tests. There is no getting around them. They come as tests of mind, body, and heart. Sometimes we see them coming; other times they sneak up on us. Immediately following his baptism, Jesus moved from the crowds around John the Baptist to the empty spaces of the wilderness. Alone, physically worn, emotionally strained, Jesus faced the tempter. Failure meant the end of his ministry and our hope. His fortitude and determination have served as examples of strength and spiritual resolve.

✶

The first three Gospels record an odd event in the life of Jesus: his temptation (Matthew 4:1-11; Mark 1:12-13; Luke 4:1-13). It is odd because of how it begins. Matthew and Luke say that the Spirit led Jesus into the wilderness. Mark uses a sharper word: *drove*. The same Holy Spirit we saw descending like a dove on Jesus at his baptism compelled him into the Judean wilderness to face his temptation. It was not accidental or unexpected. It was part of the plan.

The original word used for "wilderness" refers to a place that has been abandoned; an empty place. The geography has not changed much over the centuries. It remains a bare and rocky environment, filled with dangers. The area, northwest of Jericho, was believed to be the habitation of demons. It was not a pleasant place.

Now that Jesus has suffered and was tempted, he can help anyone else who is tempted.

Hebrews 2:18 CEV

This High Priest of ours understands our weaknesses, for he faced all of the same testings we do, yet he did not sin. So let us come boldly to the throne of our gracious God. There we will receive his mercy, and we will find grace to help us when we need it most.

Hebrews 4:15–16 NLT

There Jesus fasted forty days, his mind and heart set on God and the ministry to follow. After forty days, when Jesus was at his weakest, the

Devil came to tempt him, to test Jesus' resolve and nature. The tempter is identified as the Devil. *Devil* comes from a Greek word meaning "accuser," or "slanderer."

Three temptations are recorded. The first appealed to Jesus' physical need. The Devil said, "If You are the Son of God, command that these stones become bread" (Matthew 4:3–4 NASB). The appeal is logical. Jesus had fasted forty days and had the power to create food out of nothing. But he was there to do God's will, not the Devil's. Jesus unleashed the only weapon he had or needed: the Scriptures. Quoting from Deuteronomy 8:3, Jesus said, "Man shall not live on bread alone, but on every word that proceeds out of the mouth of God" (Matthew 4:4 NASB).

The second temptation appealed to Jesus' pride and offered a shortcut bypassing his ministry. The Devil took Jesus to the highest pinnacle of

the temple, probably a spot overlooking the deep valley that ran nearby, and encouraged Jesus to jump, reminding him that angels "will bear you up, so that you will not dash your foot against a stone" (Matthew 4:6 NRSV). What is the appeal here? The people of the day expected the Messiah to appear from the sky. Descending to the temple courtyard would cause a sensation, and Jesus would immediately be accepted before they ever heard his teaching. Jesus came to be a sacrifice for humanity, not a hero. Jesus refused, reminding the Devil with another passage from Deuteronomy that one does not "put the Lord your God to the test" (v. 7 NIV).

In the third temptation, the Devil took Jesus to a high mountain and showed him all the kingdoms of the world and offered them all to Jesus if he would just "fall down and worship" him (Matthew 4:9 NASB). That tore it. First, the Devil offered what wasn't his to give. Second, Jesus would never worship the Devil. "Go, Satan! For it is written, 'You shall worship the LORD your God, and serve Him only'" (v. 10 NASB).

The time in the wilderness, the fasting, and the temptations left Jesus physically weak. Matthew and Mark tell us that after the temptations, angels came and ministered to Jesus. It isn't difficult to imagine him too weak to walk.

Jesus didn't endure the temptations to prove himself to God. God had already shown his approval at Jesus' baptism. Nor did Jesus need to prove to Satan that he was above temptation. Most likely, the Devil had that figured out. The temptation enabled Jesus to understand the temptations we face. He went through it for our benefit.

> No temptation has seized you except what is common to man. And God is faithful; he will not let you be tempted beyond what you can bear. But when you are tempted, he will also provide a way out so that you can stand up under it.
>
> 1 Corinthians 10:13 NIV

A meaningful exercise is to compare the temptation of Jesus with the temptation of Adam and Eve in Genesis 3:1–24. Adam and Eve were tempted in a beautiful garden; Jesus was tempted in an abandoned wilderness; both were tempted with food but for different reasons; both were tempted to sacrifice God's plan for their own. Adam and Eve failed. Thankfully, Jesus didn't.

Points to Remember

Philip Yancey noted in his book *The Jesus I Never Knew* that Satan proposed "improvements" that came without cost, emphasizing the good parts of being human without having to deal with the problems. He wanted Jesus to make bread without having to work for it, to feign facing danger when no danger was present, to enjoy adulation and acceptance while avoiding rejection.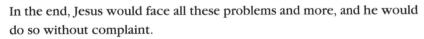
In the end, Jesus would face all these problems and more, and he would do so without complaint.

Jesus faced each temptation successfully because he found his mission more important than relief from hunger or danger.

Check Your Understanding

- **What do Jesus' actions teach us about resisting temptation in our lives?**

He showed that temptation is best resisted by seeing past it and fixing our gaze on the great goal; that the best way to fight temptation is to know and use the Scriptures; and that our response to temptation affects others.

- **Jesus lived a sinless life. Does that mean he cannot relate to our daily lives?**

The benefit of Jesus' trials is that we have a Savior who knows what it is to be tempted and, as the Bible says in Hebrews 4:15, understands what we go through.

- **After the last temptation, Jesus ordered the Devil to leave. What does that mean?**

The responsibility rests with us. Sometimes the best course of action is to remove the temptation from our presence.

- **All the temptations were aimed at felt needs: food, pride, and wealth. Do we face the same temptations?**

We do. We have a need for the basics of food and shelter; we all wish to be admired for something; and wealth is still alluring. Jesus focused on things he knew to be more important. He focused not on the present need but on the future one.

- **What does the temptation say about Jesus?**

First, that he did not come to have his needs met; he came to meet ours. Second, that everyone, including him, faces temptation—it's how we face temptation that matters. Third, Jesus would surrender temporary comfort for a greater good—a good that touches us all.

Many Names and Titles—One Person

When reading the Bible it doesn't take long to realize that Jesus is referred to by different names and many attributions. To the Hebrew mind, names were profoundly important and spoke to the character of the name-bearer. The Bible contains more than 150 names, titles, and appellations that refer to Jesus, some of which were coined by Jesus himself. These names help us understand Jesus as a person, his deity, his work, his position in our lives, and much more. The following are a few of the better-known names of Jesus.

In Romeo and Juliet, Shakespeare asked through Juliet, "What's in a name? That which we call a rose by any other name would smell as sweet." Juliet's point is that names don't make the person. Romeo would be Romeo no matter what his name. Jesus would be Jesus no matter what name we assigned to him. His many names reveal his character and goals.

Jesus. If we lived with Jesus, we would have heard him called by his Hebrew name, Yoshua (Joshua), which means "Jehovah is salvation." The name has traveled through Hebrew, Aramaic, Greek, Latin, and finally into English.

The Lord will save everyone who asks for his help.

Acts 2:21 CEV

God lifted him high and honored him far beyond anyone or anything, ever, so that all created beings in heaven and on earth— even those long ago dead and buried—will bow in worship before this Jesus Christ, and call out in praise that he is the Master of all, to the glorious honor of God the Father.

Philippians 2:9–11 MSG

Immanuel. This is an Old Testament Hebrew name that means "God is with us." It occurs in Isaiah 7:14, a prophecy of the virgin birth, and relates to Jesus' deity. When Jesus came, it was truly God stepping into human form to be among his people in a way they could understand.

Word. John uses the Greek term *Logos* to describe the preexistent Jesus—Jesus before he took on flesh. It shows Jesus as existing before creation and then entering our sphere of existence. The term *logos* refers to the spoken word. The first few verses of John remind the reader of the creation account in Genesis, where the repeated phrase "And God said" appears. Jesus is that Word.

Messiah/Christ. *Messiah* and *Christ* both mean "Anointed One." The former is Hebrew, the latter Greek. The terms refer to someone who is anointed of God. Priests and kings used to be anointed with oil, with the oil representing the presence of God. When we say, "Jesus Christ," we are referring to him by his given name and as the Anointed One of God. Jews looked for the Messiah to be a spiritual and national leader. Jesus certainly filled the first and will become the latter at the second coming.

Son of God. The phrase is used about forty times in the New Testament and reminds us that Jesus is truly God's Son. It highlights his deity. Theologians have fancy terms like *hypostatic union* to describe the melding of the divine and human nature in Jesus. It is impossible to explain, but Jesus taught that he was both divine like God and human like us. A Roman centurion standing near the cross said, "Surely this man was the Son of God!" (Mark 15:39 NIV). He was right in general and wrong on one point: Jesus was and *is* the Son of God. That never changes.

Son of Man. Used approximately eighty-five times in the New Testament, it was Jesus' favorite term for himself. He used it because it emphasized his connection to humanity. Jesus never downplayed his humanity. Although it was quite a step down from what he experienced in heaven, he always used the phrase *Son of Man* with honor and pride.

Chief Shepherd. Peter referred to Jesus (1 Peter 5:4 NASB) as "the Chief Shepherd," a phrase that reminded his readers of Jesus' self-description as the good shepherd who lays down his life for his sheep (John 10:11). Today, the title conjures up a loving, dedicated person, but shepherds were outcasts of the day. Sheep were needed, but the shepherds who attended them were considered the lowest class.

First and Last. Revelation, the last book in the New Testament, is a record of the apostle John's epic vision in which Jesus appeared to him and unveiled much of the future. In that vision Jesus said, "I am the Alpha and the Omega, the First and the Last, the Beginning and the End" (Revelation 22:13 NIV)—three self-descriptions that show Jesus' eternal nature. There was never a time when Jesus wasn't; there will never be a time when Jesus isn't. The "Alpha and the Omega" phrase refers to the Greek alphabet, which begins with *alpha* and ends with *omega*. It's the same as saying, "I am the A and the Z."

> This shows that the Son is far greater than the angels, just as the name God gave him is far greater than their names.
>
> Hebrews 1:4 NLT

Digging Deeper

There's another revealing name for Jesus. This one exposes not only something about Jesus, but also something about our relationship to him. *Lord* is a dual-purpose word often used to mean "sir," but the word also is often used for anyone with authority, superiority, and command. When used in reference to Jesus, it usually is used in the second sense. When we speak of Jesus as Lord, we are saying that he has authority over our lives, an authority we surrender to him. We elevate him above ourselves and submit to his teaching. He's not just *a* Lord, but *the* Lord.

Final Thought

Why are there more than 150 names, descriptors, and titles for Jesus? It is because no single term can do him justice. Language—all languages—is self-limiting. He is King and Shepherd, Messiah and Servant, and many things more. Perhaps 150 names are not enough.

Check Your Understanding

- We use titles to describe the work people do. Titles such as doctor and professor give us some insight. What do the titles listed for Jesus teach us about him?

His names and titles show us that he is God, man, preexistent, and Lord of our lives.

- It is interesting that Jesus' favorite term for himself was Son of Man. Why do you suppose that was?

Most people want to be known by their most impressive qualities; Jesus wanted to be known for his love for humankind.

- Why does the Bible record so many names for Jesus?

He is larger than any single term can define. He has done more than any single description can record, because there has never been anyone like him.

Jesus at the Temple—Unafraid of Confrontation

If you ask most people to describe Jesus in one word, they will likely say meek. *It would be a good description if not for the basic misunderstanding we have of the word. Meek does mean mild-mannered and humble, but it does not mean weak. The words sound similar but have nothing to do with each other. Weakness is a lack of physical, mental, or moral strength. Meekness is quiet strength, the kind of power Jesus displayed one day at the temple.*

✳

Passover festivities were in full swing, and thousands had traveled from every corner of the kingdom to worship in Jerusalem. Passover was the greatest religious holiday of the time, and much of the activity took place close to a magnificent structure called the temple. Around the central building were several courts, each designated for a particular group of people: Gentiles, women, Jewish men. Only priests could enter the temple itself.

Many travelers had to buy sacrificial animals, and the prices could be steep. In addition, every Jew had to pay the half-shekel tax, and payment had to be made with a Jewish coin. Moneychangers exchanged Roman money for Jewish coins—for a high price. Part of the temple area had been converted into a center of commerce.

Disgusted, Jesus constructed a whip from cords, drove the animals out, and overturned the moneychangers' tables. "Take these things away; stop making My Father's house a place of business" (John 2:16 NASB).

It is zeal for your house that has consumed me; the insults of those who insult you have fallen on me.

Psalm 69:9 NRSV

He found people selling cattle, sheep, and doves in the temple. He also saw moneychangers sitting at their tables. So he took some rope and made a whip. Then he chased everyone out of the temple, together with their sheep and cattle. He turned over the tables of the moneychangers and scattered their coins.

John 2:14–15 CEV

The Jewish leaders wanted a sign proving he had the authority to do such a thing. His sign was a comment: "Destroy this temple, and in three days I will raise it up" (John 2:19 NASB). Most likely, he pointed to himself when he made the statement. It's the earliest personal reference to his resurrection. Of course, the religious leaders thought he meant the temple complex and scoffed.

Jesus began his ministry with confrontation. He purified the temple area to allow Jews and Gentiles freedom to worship. Commercialism is nothing new. Jesus faced it two thousand years ago.

Final Thought

The image many have of Jesus as the weak, doormat Messiah is wrong. Jesus saw a religious crime and addressed it. He never shied away from necessary confrontation. The religious leaders allowed activity that was offensive to God and to respectful worshippers. He decided it was time for a change.

Check Your Understanding

- **Does knowing that *meek* doesn't mean "weak" change your image of Jesus?**

Having the correct image of Jesus is important. On several occasions he confronted his critics—those who abused others with laws and traditions, and even his own disciples when necessary.

- **Does knowing that Jesus could be confrontational detract from his image?**

It shouldn't. All that Jesus did, he did in love and for the good of those around him. His confrontations were honest but never self-serving or demeaning to others. His confrontations were never unthinking reactions but were reasoned corrections.

How Jesus Lived Sinless in a World of Sinners

Sin has always been an unpopular word, and yet few people would say they lived a sinless life. Only one person can make that claim and be correct. Jesus lived without sin. Facing temptations as we do, it might seem impossible for a man to live more than three decades and not sin. This seems even more improbable when we realize that every person he met was a sinner. In the course of human history, he alone lived without sinning. Jesus faced more temptations than those he experienced in the wilderness, and yet he remained spotless.

A student in Bible college finished four years of study and, as the last step to his graduation, sat before several members of the faculty "defending" his doctrinal statement. One of the faculty members attempted to draw him into theological debate about whether or not it was possible for Jesus to sin. The student thought then said, "The only answer that matters is he didn't."

The Bible makes it clear that everyone sins. "Everyone has sinned; we all fall short of God's glorious standard" (Romans 3:23 NLT). This idea is repeated many times. By contrast, the Bible also makes it clear that Jesus never sinned. "You know that he appeared so that he might take away our sins. And in him is no sin" (1 John 3:5 NIV).

Jesus came to accomplish many things, but most of all he came to be the sacrifice for our sin. It's a difficult thought to grasp, but it is nonetheless true. To be the perfect sacri-

Christ never sinned! But God treated him as a sinner, so that Christ could make us acceptable to God.

2 Corinthians 5:21 CEV

Who would dare tangle with God by messing with one of God's chosen? Who would dare even to point a finger? The One who died for us—who was raised to life for us!—is in the presence of God at this very moment sticking up for us.

Romans 8:33–34 MSG

fice, he had to be sinless. His sinless life also makes us aware of our own sin and gives us a desire to live as purely as Jesus did.

One might expect a sinless person to feel arrogance around sinful people, but Jesus never showed such prejudice. He preferred the company of the faulty. One of the earliest charges laid against him by the religious leaders was that he befriended sinners. Jesus showed no shame at the accusation. Sinners were welcome in his presence.

Final Thought

 Sin brings shame. Jesus takes us as we are and loves us anyway. The apostle Paul wrote, "God demonstrates His own love toward us, in that while we were still sinners, Christ died for us" (Romans 5:7-8 NKJV). The only sinless person loved sinners enough to die for them.

Check Your Understanding

- **What could cause a sinless Jesus to befriend sinners like unbelievers, prostitutes, and others?**

Love is the only force that can bridge such a gap. Jesus didn't look at what people were but saw what they could be with a relation to God through him.

- **The ability to resist sin is based in the desire to achieve something greater than the sin itself. How does that work in a person's life?**

If we love something more than our sin, then we'll leave sin behind. A commitment to Jesus is more desirable than whatever tempts us.

Suffocated by Crowds— Jesus Dealt with the Masses

In Sir Andrew Lloyd Webber's musical *Jesus Christ Superstar,* countless men and women afflicted with disease press in upon Jesus. They cry, "See me stand, I can hardly walk," and "See my eyes, I can hardly see." More and more of the afflicted mob Jesus. The work catches a bit of what it must have been like. Once the miracles began, thousands would come out to him, many with pressing needs. One of Jesus' greatest challenges was dealing with the people who mobbed him, each demanding something from him.

A young pastor went to visit a child at Children's Hospital in San Diego. He had been in hospitals, but this was his first time in a facility devoted to children. Through open doors, he saw the bald heads of six-year-olds with cancer, a ten-year-old with both legs in traction, a young girl wearing an oxygen mask, and more. Before he knew it, he had diverted his eyes to the hall floor. Within moments of his arrival, he had stopped looking.

Jesus' teaching and his miracles drew people to him. The lame walked, the blind regained sight, the lepers were made whole. Soon Jesus and his disciples were awash in human need forcing them from one place to another. In one case, Jesus was teaching in a home in Capernaum (Mark 2:1–5). The crowd was so great that there was no room in the house. Four men brought a paralyzed man on a pallet to see Jesus, but they couldn't get close to him. The inventive four carried their

Great multitudes followed Him — from Galilee, and from Decapolis, Jerusalem, Judea, and beyond the Jordan.

Matthew 4:25 NKJV

When he saw the crowds, he felt sorry for them. They were confused and helpless, like sheep without a shepherd.

Matthew 9:36 CEV

friend onto the flat roof and dug through the roofing material so they could lower the man to Jesus. Jesus healed him, and he walked from the scene.

The crowds show us the popularity of Jesus, but more important, they show Jesus' commitment to those seeking him. Jesus' purpose wasn't to heal every sickness. The miracles proved his claims but were not the center of his mission. Still, Jesus rewarded faith wherever he found it.

Take It to Heart

 It's difficult to look on pain and sorrow. Most of us would rather turn away, yet a part of us knows that we shouldn't. Jesus faced such things every day, and seldom did they come one at a time. Jesus, sometimes at great emotional cost to himself, brought hope to the crowds.

Check Your Understanding

- **Besides the miracles and the teaching, were there other reasons crowds followed Jesus?**

The people were oppressed on two fronts: the Romans and the religious leaders. Jesus' teaching offered a freedom that could be found nowhere else. He didn't bring new religious laws; he brought the promise of a relationship with God.

- **Do you suppose Jesus felt drained by the crowds?**

Reading the Gospels reveals that the crowds exacted an emotional toll from Jesus. Additionally, Jesus had to employ creative methods just to be heard.

Jesus' Need to Get Away

The need to be alone is wired into our human nature. When life's pressures settle on our shoulders, when we feel ill, and when we're under stress, we long for some alone time. Jesus was no different. His work was demanding, emotional, and dangerous. From time to time, he withdrew from the public eye, moving into less-populated areas to be alone. Sometimes he took his disciples with him; other times he wanted absolute solitude, time to be away from the constant tug of the crowds and the criticism of the religious leaders.

✳

The Gospels record several times when Jesus pulled away to be with his disciples or to be alone. As with us, there were often reasons that prompted the retreat.

Threats against his life. Jesus faced more danger than most realized. A segment of religious leaders found Jesus' message offensive. Even more offensive were the large crowds that followed him. Jesus had supplanted them in the eyes of the people. Fearful of their ever-eroding loss of influence, they turned to murder plots. Upon hearing a new threat, Jesus would retreat from the area (Matthew 12:14–15).

Death of John the Baptist. John the Baptist was imprisoned and later beheaded by Herod. The news of the Baptist's death hit Jesus hard, and he traveled to a solitary place (Matthew 14:13). But a large crowd followed, with the sick looking for healing. Jesus didn't have time to grieve.

> Very early in the morning, while it was still dark, Jesus got up, left the house and went off to a solitary place, where he prayed. Simon and his companions went to look for him, and when they found him, they exclaimed: "Everyone is looking for you!"
>
> Mark 1:35–37 NIV
>
> When Jesus saw that they were ready to force him to be their king, he slipped away into the hills by himself.
>
> John 6:15 NLT

Prayer. Luke 5:16 says that Jesus often withdrew to lonely places and prayed. Jesus didn't want to be alone; he wanted to be alone with God. These were times when Jesus could rest and recharge his batteries. Even Jesus needed rest.

Teaching his disciples. The disciples would one day take the message of Jesus to the world. Consequently, they needed special instruction, something difficult to achieve when constantly surrounded by scores of attention-needy people. Withdrawing with Jesus, his "team" had time to rest and sit at his feet.

Final Thought

 The actress Greta Garbo said, "I want to be alone." Later she clarified: "I said I want to be *let* alone. There's a difference." Jesus withdrew because it was necessary. It is good for us to withdraw for time alone, time to pray, time to think, and time to plan.

Check Your Understanding

- **Was it selfish for Jesus to withdraw from the people who were seeking his help?**

No. Jesus was fully man, which meant he felt fatigue, hunger, and everything else that we feel. Withdrawing for a time would allow him to continue his work. Sometimes withdrawing is the best thing we can do for others.

- **Jesus never withdrew because he ceased loving people. How can we know that statement is true?**

Jesus always returned to his work and mission and continued all the way to the cross.

"I Am"—How Jesus Described Himself

Jesus made approximately 170 claims about himself, claims that no one else could truthfully make. All but one described his many functions, and one clarified his nature.

While many great men and women can describe themselves by their accomplishments, the positions they hold, or discoveries they've made, none could rightly claim to be the Savior of the world and follow it up with teachings and actions the prove the point.

Jesus' self-revelation included blunt statements, inferences, agreement with conclusions drawn by others, and metaphors. The Gospel of John records a special type of self-description: the "I am" statement.

I am the bread of life" (John 6:35 NLT). One of the most remarkable miracles was the feeding of more than five thousand people. Jesus took five small loaves of bread and two small fish and multiplied them for the weary crowd until everyone had eaten their fill. He later left, and the crowd found him the next morning on the other side of a lake. The crowd asked for a sign, and they brought up the manna God sent to support the Hebrews during their forty years of wandering. It came across as a hint for more food. Jesus said, "I am the bread of life," then explained that he is the means to eternal life. He drew a parallel between the manna of Moses' day and himself: "I am the bread that came down from heaven" (v. 41 NIV). Manna gave life to the people of the exodus; Jesus gives eternal life to all who believe in him.

Jesus said to them, "Very truly, I tell you, before Abraham was, I am."

John 8:58 NRSV

God said to Moses: I am the eternal God. So tell them that the LORD, whose name is " I Am," has sent you.

Exodus 3:14 CEV

"I am the light of the world" (John 8:12; 9:5 NLT). This phrase follows the episode of the woman caught in adultery. Religious leaders brought the woman in order to trap Jesus. Mosaic law taught that the woman should be stoned to death, but Jesus' kindness was already well known. Jesus answered, "He who is without sin among you, let him throw a stone at her first" (8:7 NKJV). The accusers left, and he turned his attention to the crowd. "I am the light of the world. He who follows Me shall not walk in darkness, but have the light of life" (8:12 NKJV). Jesus claimed to be the light in a world of darkness, and not just any light, but the light that brought life.

"I am the gate" (John 10:7 NIV). Jesus taught with stories and sometimes used metaphors. He painted a picture everyone of that day would recognize. Shepherds sometimes kept sheep in corrals during the night for safety. The animals would pass in and out of an opening in a stone wall that the shepherd controlled. Jesus said he was the gate through which the sheep (his followers) passed. What did he mean? He is the passageway to security and eternal safety. The corral kept predators out. The only way to the sheep was through the gate. Our only way to God's provision is through Jesus.

"I am the good shepherd" (John 10:11 NKJV). Jesus called himself the good shepherd. Shepherds were not highly regarded and were not welcome in certain ranks of society, but Jesus saw no shame in associating himself with them. Shepherds cared for and protected the sheep, leading them to pasture and then back to the safety of a particular area or stone corral. Jesus watches over his followers.

"I am the resurrection and the life" (John 11:25 NIV). When Jesus uttered these words, he did so to a grieving Martha, who mourned the death of her brother, Lazarus. Jesus said, "I am the resurrection and the life; he who believes in Me will live even if he dies" (11:25 NASB). Jesus would be the first true resurrection. Although others have been brought back to life (as in this passage), they all died again. When Jesus rose from the grave, it was forever. That all believers would someday be resurrected is a part of Jesus' message to the ages.

"I am the way, and the truth, and the life" (John 14:6 NASB). In this one line, Jesus made three statements about himself. He is the way (the road); the truth about all things spiritual; and the one who gives eternal life.

"I am the vine" (John 15:5 NLT). One of the major crops of Jesus' day was grapes, some of which were used for food and others for wine. This metaphor shows Jesus as the grapevine from which the fruit-bearing branches draw the nourishment they need to survive and produce. Without the vine, the branches are useless. Jesus' followers are connected to him in a vital, life-giving way.

Digging Deeper

Revelation is a record of a vision experienced by John. Like the Gospel of John, it contains several "I am" statements (1:17; 1:18; 21:6; 22:13; 22:16). One of the best known is "I am the Alpha and the Omega" (Revelation 1:8 NIV). Alpha is the first letter of the Greek alphabet; Omega is the last. Jesus used this phrase three times  in the book. He also described himself as the living One who was dead but now alive forever (1:18). In the last "I am" statement, Jesus called himself "the Root and the Offspring of David, the Bright and Morning Star" (22:16 NKJV), indicating that he is the Messiah.

Final Thought

Jesus went to great lengths to describe himself in a way people could understand. He did not do so because of his ego, but because such knowledge is crucial to our understanding of his mission and to distinguish himself from other teachers. Having the right view of Jesus makes all the difference.

Check Your Understanding

- Many of us describe ourselves by our occupations. After hearing some of the "I am" statements, how might someone describe Jesus' occupation?

As the Way, the Truth, the Life, the Good Shepherd, the Gate, and the other descriptions, it is easy to see that Jesus' occupation was to draw us back to God.

- If we didn't have the context of the Gospels, it might be easy to mistake Jesus' statements as arrogance. How do we know it's not his ego talking?

Each statement shows us that Jesus' ministry was focused on our spiritual needs.

- Each "I am" statement is meant to show Jesus as different from the prevailing idea of faith. How do they achieve this?

Each statement shows that salvation doesn't come by good works or legalism but through the sacrifice of Jesus.

"Who Do People Say I Am?"

Twenty centuries ago, Jesus put a question to the disciples that is still asked around the world. It may be the most important question ever asked: "Who do people say I am?" After two thousand years the debate still rages—which is odd since Jesus and Peter settled it in a town at the base of the Hebron Mountains. Jesus and his disciples withdrew to an area about twenty-five miles north of the Sea of Galilee. There he could focus on his disciples and take them to the next level. He did so with two questions.

✳

Away from the pressing crowds, in the cooler air near the mountains, Jesus asked, "Who do people say that the Son of Man is?" (Matthew 16:13 NRSV). It was a simple question with a life-changing answer.

The disciples' answer is revealing. "Some say John the Baptist, but others Elijah, and still others Jeremiah or one of the prophets" (Matthew 16:14 NRSV). After all the miracles, the authoritative teaching, the terms Jesus used to describe himself, people still chose to believe Jesus was the executed John the Baptist or one of the Old Testament prophets.

Jesus asked the question in a more personal way, "But who do you say that I am?" (Matthew 16:15 NASB). Peter answered for the group. "You are the Messiah, the Son of the living God" (v. 16 NLT).

The crowds even got into an argument about him. Some were saying, "Jesus is a good man," while others were saying, "He is lying to everyone."

John 7:12 CEV

The Roman officer and the other soldiers at the crucifixion were terrified by the earthquake and all that had happened. They said, "This man truly was the Son of God!"

Matthew 27:54 NLT

Jesus' response was filled with emotion. He praised Peter, calling him blessed, and then said Peter's answer came from God the Father. The key is in that statement. Recognizing Jesus is more than an academic exercise. It involves a spiritual insight.

Jesus has been described as a myth, a mentally unbalanced man, a good man, a teacher, a rabbi, and a prophet. Jesus is so much more. C. S. Lewis said Jesus was either a liar, a lunatic, or Lord: a liar if he said the things he did but knew they were false; a lunatic if he believed he was the Messiah but wasn't; but if he was everything he claimed to be, then he must be Lord.

Final Thought

Jesus made some amazing claims about himself. These claims can be accepted or rejected. Every person gets to make that choice. Centuries of discussion and examination have led many to the inescapable conclusion that Jesus was everything he claimed to be.

Check Your Understanding

- **Peter's answer was that Jesus was the Messiah. Why do you suppose Jesus reacted with such praise?**

Jesus reacted that way because Peter had crossed a threshold of understanding and was willing to make a public statement about his belief.

- **Why do you think the people were so confused about who Jesus was?**

We all have a tendency to force puzzling things into familiar molds. Also, they were expecting a conquering Messiah, and Jesus didn't fit their preconceptions.

The Emotional Jesus—The Times Jesus Wept

It's the shortest verse in the English Bible. Just two words: "Jesus wept" (John 11:35 NLT). That's it, but it carries a lot of meaning. On several occasions Jesus is said to have wept or been moved with compassion. The Greek word for compassion *means "to be churned up." Those who have received tragic news often clutch at their stomachs and double over. That's the meaning of the word. Emotion is not merely mental—it's physical. Jesus expressed many emotions, including sorrow and compassion.*

✳

The English word *emotion* is a compound word meaning "to be moved within." The root of *emotion* is "motion," and Jesus knew what it meant to feel the raw impact of sadness. The scene took place in Bethany just outside the family tomb of Mary, Martha, and Lazarus. Jesus often visited their home, which was a short distance from Jerusalem. There seems to have been a close connection between the siblings and Jesus.

Lazarus fell ill and died. Jews buried their dead as soon as possible, usually the same day. Jesus arrived four days after Lazarus had been entombed. Others joined Jesus at the tomb, including Martha. Sadness filled the air. Jesus wept.

The irony of the account is that Jesus would bring Lazarus back to life. The dead man in the tomb would

When the city came into view, he wept over it. "If you had only recognized this day, and everything that was good for you! But now it's too late."

Luke 19:41–42 MSG

Filled with compassion, Jesus reached out his hand and touched the man. "I am willing," he said. "Be clean!" Immediately the leprosy left him and he was cured.

Mark 1:41–42 NIV

soon walk out. Nevertheless, Jesus wept. Why? Most scholars put forth one of two ideas. First, Jesus wept because he not only sympathized but empathized with Martha and the others. Second, he wept because he would be bringing Lazarus back from a better place. Both ideas may be true. The point is, Jesus bore the same emotions as any human, and he wasn't ashamed to express them.

Jesus could have said, "People die. It's part of life." He could have remained aloof, but instead he chose the difficult emotion. The moment moved him, and he joined the others in their sorrow. Christians believe he does the same for us today.

Points to Remember

Jesus never avoided the uncomfortable emotion of others or the deep emotions that churned within him. Jesus was different from those around him; in an equal number of ways, he was the same. Jesus isn't a distant Savior but one who understands what we feel.

Check Your Understanding

- When we feel sorry for someone, we call it sympathy. When we truly understand the emotions of another, we call it empathy. What does it mean that Jesus was empathetic?

It means that Jesus not only sees when we hurt, he hurts with us. The same can be said for our joy.

- While Jesus displayed his emotions, he didn't let emotions control his actions. What lesson does that hold for us?

Emotions can be misleading. Genuine emotions are helpful but should never override reason and wisdom.

Jesus Came for Reasons Different Than Expected

Expectations can be enjoyable, but they can also be misleading. Jesus' arrival and ministry are well known to us today, but in the first century, expectations had religious leaders and everyday people looking for something different. As we've noted, the Jews of Jesus' day were oppressed, first by the occupying Romans but also by overbearing religious leaders. Jesus fulfilled the Old Testament prophecies for the coming of the Messiah, but expectations had many looking for someone different. Consequently, many missed the very person they were looking for.

An interesting thing happens in the book of Acts. Acts was written by Luke, the same man who wrote the Gospel of Luke. While the name "Jesus" and the title "Christ" are found in the Gospels, the number of times the words are linked increases dramatically in Acts. Peter made it official in Caesarea Philippi with his proclamation that Jesus was the Christ, the Son of the living God, but the people who acknowledged the fact were few.

> While we were still weak, at the right time Christ died for the ungodly. Indeed, rarely will anyone die for a righteous person—though perhaps for a good person someone might actually dare to die.
>
> Romans 5:6–7 NRSV

> This is how God showed his love for us: God sent his only Son into the world so we might live through him.
>
> 1 John 4:9 MSG

After Jesus' death, resurrection, and ascension, the ministry passed to the disciples. Peter preached his first sermon (Acts 2:14–37), and it was a scorcher. Peter pulled no punches. The theme of his sermon was simple: Jesus is the Christ (Messiah). "There's no longer room for doubt—God made him Master and Messiah, this Jesus whom you killed on a cross" (Acts 2:36 MSG).

Jesus came not as a conquering Messiah but as a suffering one. Why? No one can blame the people for wanting to be free of Roman oppression, but they had a great need, one that went beyond governmental and earthly desires: they needed spiritual freedom. Jesus described his ministry several times. "The Son of Man has come to seek and to save that which was lost" (Luke 19:10 NKJV).

Wants and needs are often at odds. Jesus came to give us what we need, not what we expect.

Points to Remember

Jesus could have fulfilled the people's desires but would have had to bypass the thing they really needed: a way to reunite with God. Jesus came as a suffering Messiah in lieu of a conquering one. He chose to associate with the poor, teach eternal truths, die, and be resurrected.

Check Your Understanding

- **Expectations are bad only if they prevent us from seeing more important things, such as our spiritual lives. How do expectations blind us to needs?**

Expectations are as powerful as they are common. Expectations are often rooted in desire rather than wisdom. We each should ask, What are my real needs?

- **There are many opinions about Jesus that don't match his history or work. What misguided expectations do people have of Jesus today?**

Some believe that Jesus was an ancient man who has no relevance today; that spiritual solutions are unnecessary.

Jesus Is More Than He Seems—Transfiguration

When read for the first time, it sounds like something from *The X-Files* or *The Outer Limits*: three men in mysterious form, three witnesses, and a voice from heaven. Add a glowing cloud so strange it frightens grown men, and we have the ingredients for an eerie television script. Except in this case, we're talking about a historical event, not the product of a writer's mind. The transfiguration of Christ, as revealing as it is astonishing, was unlike any other event in history (Matthew 17:1–13; Mark 9:1–13; Luke 9:28–36).

Late in the third year of Jesus' ministry, he ascended a mountain with three of his closest disciples. After a tiring walk, the disciples settled in to rest. Luke noted the men were sleeping when the event began. When they opened their eyes, they beheld a very different-looking Jesus talking to two men.

First, they noticed Jesus' appearance seemed to be altered. Matthew and Mark use the word *metamorphosis*, which refers to something that has physically changed. His face shone like a light. In fact, we get our word *lamp* from the Greek word used to describe Jesus' face. His clothing changed into something that gleamed and dazzled.

As if that weren't enough, two men stood with Jesus—men the disciples recognized as Moses and Elijah.

We did not follow cleverly invented stories when we told you about the power and coming of our Lord Jesus Christ, but we were eyewitnesses of his majesty. For he received honor and glory from God the Father when the voice came to him from the Majestic Glory, saying, "This is my Son, whom I love; with him I am well pleased." We ourselves heard this voice that came from heaven when we were with him on the sacred mountain.

2 Peter 1:16–18 NIV

We have seen and testify that the Father has sent the Son to be the Savior of the world.

1 John 4:14 NASB

How did they identify two men who died many centuries before? No one knows. Perhaps they overheard Jesus use their names. Perhaps Jesus introduced them. Maybe they learned the two men's identities by divine revelation. We can only guess.

God had chosen Moses to deliver the Hebrews kept for centuries in Egyptian slavery; Elijah was one of the greatest prophets. Elijah had another distinction: the Bible lists two men who never died—Enoch (Genesis 5:24) and Elijah (2 Kings 2:11).

The disciples overheard at least part of the conversation. Luke records that Jesus, Moses, and Elijah were "speaking of His departure which He was about to accomplish at Jerusalem" (Luke 9:31 NASB). There is an interesting play on words in the original language. The word translated *departure* comes from the Greek word *exodus*, which means "exit." *Exodus* is the word we use to describe the massive migration of the Hebrews from Egypt to the Promised Land.

Elijah had a spectacular exit of his own. At the conclusion of his ministry, Elijah was taken up into heaven in a fiery chariot. In some ways, his exit foreshadowed Jesus' ascension into heaven. There would be no fiery chariot, but Jesus would nonetheless ascend skyward in full view of witnesses.

What kind of exodus would Jesus lead? Two types. First, the word *exodus* used by Luke is often used the same way we use the word *deceased*. They were talking about Jesus' pending death in Jerusalem. Jesus' death, however, was not the end of the story or the end of Jesus. Jesus would die, but he would also be bodily resurrected. There was another type of exodus Jesus would lead: the faithful to heaven. Years later, the apostle Paul would write a letter to the church at Ephesus. In it, he quoted the Old Testament book of Psalms (68:18): "When He ascended on high, He led captive a host of captives, and He gave gifts to men" (Ephesians 4:8 NASB). Those words were written a thousand years before Jesus' time, but they captured a part of God's plan. Jesus came to free the captives. That's us. And he leads his followers to a Promised Land, not the earthly land to which Moses led the Israelites, but an eternal land called heaven.

The three disciples couldn't believe their eyes. To see Jesus transformed and recognize two of the most famous people from their Jewish past overwhelmed them. They were ready to stay there forever. As they spoke, a cloud formed over them and surrounded everyone, terrifying the disciples. Then a voice: "This is my Son, whom I have chosen; listen to him" (Luke 9:35 NIV). When the cloud dissipated, Moses and Elijah were gone.

> After six days Jesus took Peter, James, and John his brother, led them up on a high mountain by themselves; and He was transfigured before them. His face shone like the sun, and His clothes became as white as the light.
>
> Matthew 17:1–2 NKJV

Why this display? Some have suggested that Moses and Elijah were there to encourage Jesus to continue on to the cross, but there is no indication that he planned to do otherwise. A close look at the scene shows the transfiguration wasn't for Jesus' benefit, but for the disciples' and, by extension, for us. The disciples struggled with Jesus' true identity. On that mountain, their doubts were put to rest. Jesus was the Messiah, the Son of God.

Digging Deeper

Having Moses and Elijah there reminds us that life continues. Moses died 1,400 years before, and Elijah disappeared 850 years prior, but that day the disciples saw them as living persons—proof that life continues on after death. The lesson for the disciples was simple: Jesus was neither Elijah nor Moses; he was and is someone far greater. The lesson for us is the same. Jesus is more than we can ever imagine. God's own testimony was that Jesus was his Son. That should end all debate. There is life after death, and Jesus is the one who made that possible.

Final Thoughts

The three disciples would have happily stayed, but Jesus didn't give them that opportunity. Jerusalem, with the horrors of the cross, awaited Jesus so he led the three back into the normal world. We do the same. We take the mountaintop experiences into the world so others can benefit.

Check Your Understanding

- **How many people were at the Mount of Transfiguration? (Careful, it's a trick question.)**

A perfect seven: Peter, James, and John; Jesus, Elijah, and Moses; and God (as represented by the voice and the cloud).

- **Is there some reason why Jesus would wait until late in his ministry to participate in this event?**

Yes. Jesus was nearing the time of his betrayal, trials, and crucifixion. It was important for the disciples to know who Jesus was and what he would achieve in leading the believers' "exodus" in the weeks ahead.

- **How do you suppose the three disciples felt at having to leave the mountain after seeing the transfiguration?**

They probably felt a mixture of emotions. They had seen something no one else had and felt a longing to stay on that spot, but Jesus led them back to the difficult world in which they lived, so they must have felt sadness.

How Jesus Worked

Preacher, teacher, prophet, healer, leader. Jesus is unique, and that uniqueness makes him the most significant person to have ever lived. Jesus changes lives, and each miracle he performed was a testimony to his power and presence.

Contents

Jesus went about all Galilee, teaching in their synagogues, preaching the gospel of the kingdom, and healing all kinds of sickness and all kinds of disease among the people.

Matthew 4:23 NKJV

Jesus the Itinerant Preacher

In a day of mass communications, it is difficult for us to understand how Jesus achieved all he did without television, radio, a publishing company, marketing, and advertising. The most influential man touched the world without ever leaving his own small country. People traveled great distances to hear him speak; crowds followed him for days, leaving work and homes behind. Jesus never held a microphone, and yet thousands hung on his every word. Today evangelists form nonprofit organizations, raise funds, set up Web pages, and more. Jesus just walked and taught.

Jesus was an itinerant preacher who traveled on foot from town to town and spoke to those who would listen. Most of Jesus' ministry took place in a land that was approximately 150 miles long north to south and an average of 70 miles wide.

There were several basic areas of the country, but Jesus spent most of his time in four of them: Galilee in the north, Judea in the south, Samaria sandwiched between them, and Perea to the east. Jesus spent much of his ministry in Galilee, but he traveled to Jerusalem in the south several times.

He said to them, "Let us go into the next towns, that I may preach there also, because for this purpose I have come forth."

Mark 1:38 NKJV

The Spirit of the Lord is upon me, because he has anointed me to bring good news to the poor. He has sent me to proclaim release to the captives and recovery of sight to the blind, to let the oppressed go free, to proclaim the year of the Lord's favor.

Luke 4:18–19 NRSV

Considering Jesus' ministry lasted only three years, it is remarkable how much of the country he covered. He walked from town to town teaching, leaving when the crowds or the danger grew too great. When a teacher of the law said, "Teacher, I will follow you wherever you go," Jesus replied, "Foxes have holes and birds of the air have nests, but the Son of Man has no place to lay his head" (Matthew 8:19–20 NIV). In other words, during his ministry, Jesus had no permanent home. The life was hard.

Men and women supported Jesus much as churches are supported today. Some people opened their homes to Jesus; others provided financial support (Luke 8:3).

Jesus was an innovative teacher. Sometimes he taught in homes, but when the crowds grew too large he would teach from hillsides or, when by the Sea of Galilee, from a boat. Both conditions provided natural amplification.

Final Thought

In three short years, Jesus turned the world upside down. He did so without a marketing team or fund-raisers. His method involved going to the people, performing miracles, teaching truth, and moving on. He walked dusty roads, and he endured harsh weather and dangerous conditions to bring a message of hope.

Check Your Understanding

- **By today's standards, some would consider Jesus a failure. He acquired no personal wealth but changed the world nonetheless. What does this say about his priorities?**

Jesus' priorities were always to bring good news to all who would listen and believe. Personal comfort and wealth were never part of his formula.

- **Jesus' ministry might be described as one of minimums. Would it have worked any other way?**

Doubtful. Jesus was born in humble circumstances, and he conducted his life and ministry in a humble fashion. Such an attitude made him approachable by both the rich and the poor.

Loving What Society Rejects—Lepers and Others

A survey of Jesus' thirty-five miracles shows some intriguing behavior. In some cases, Jesus healed with the touch of a hand; in other cases, he didn't raise a finger, his very command being enough to get the job done. In several cases, he dealt with society's untouchables, those people who had been driven from their daily lives by disease, cut off from human contact. Jesus, however, didn't consider anyone untouchable. He dealt with those people through sermons without words, proving that Jesus was more interested in including people than in excluding them.

Few groups of people in the New Testament led more tragic lives than lepers did. Leprosy (today called Hansen's disease) was one of the most devastating diseases in Jesus' day. The term *leprosy* was used to describe a number of skin diseases. Almost any skin disorder could be classified as leprosy, affecting the individual's life for the rest of his days.

The human factor of leprosy was heartrending. Anyone afflicted with the disease was forbidden contact with everyone except other lepers. A man could not touch his wife or children, could not work his trade, could not attend synagogue or go to temple. If someone approached, the leper was required to shout, "Unclean! Unclean!" The loss and loneliness must have been maddening.

Soak me in your laundry and I'll come out clean, scrub me and I'll have a snow-white life.

Psalm 51:7 MSG

If we are living in the light, as God is in the light, then we have fellowship with each other, and the blood of Jesus, his Son, cleanses us from all sin.

1 John 1:7 NLT

Matthew 8:2–4 gives the account of a leper who went to Jesus. "A leper came to Him and bowed down before Him, and said, 'Lord, if You are willing, You can make me clean'" (v. 2 NASB). Such an approach violated the law. It was an act of desperation. He had heard of Jesus' miracles and turned to him as a last resort. It's beyond imagination now, but this simple act could have led to his stoning.

What did society expect Jesus to do? To back away. To order him to leave. To pick up stones and pelt the man. Jesus did none of that. Instead, he did the unexpected, the shocking, the unthinkable—he touched the man. It wasn't just a slight touch. The original word means to handle, grasp, or touch firmly. Jesus had no reluctance and said, "I am willing," and this he did in full view of others.

By the laws of the day, Jesus had just made himself unclean, meaning he could not participate in any religious activities, and the people might have held him to that standard had not the miraculous happened.

Why would Jesus do this? A study of his miracles shows he had the power to heal over distance. He could simply have commanded that the man be well, and the leprosy would have miraculously been gone. But Jesus purposefully touched the man. That simple gesture said more than can be said in a hundred books and a thousand sermons. No one was too contaminated for his love.

What the world found repulsive, Jesus found worthwhile. Jesus saw a man worthy of his help and healed his body, but he also freed him to return to his life.

Jesus healed ten lepers while traveling from Galilee to Jerusalem. The men obeyed the law and called to him from a distance, pleading for healing. Jesus ordered them to show themselves to the priest to prove they had been healed. It's interesting to compare the two healings. The first man approached Jesus despite the laws, and Jesus touched him; the others called at a distance in accordance with the law, and Jesus didn't touch them. In both cases, however, healing took place.

Another untouchable went to Jesus (Luke 8:43–48). As Jesus walked, a crowd followed, surrounding him on all sides. In the crowd was a woman who suffered a disorder that caused her to bleed. No one knows her exact condition, but most likely she had uncontrolled vaginal bleeding. This made her ceremonially unclean. Like the lepers, she was an untouchable. Anything she touched would be declared unclean. This explains her actions, because she didn't ask to be healed. She sneaked up on Jesus and touched his garment. She believed that such an act would heal her, and healed she was.

> Christ sacrificed his life's blood to set us free, which means that our sins are now forgiven. Christ did this because God was so kind to us. God has great wisdom and understanding.
>
> Ephesians 1:7–8 CEV

This was a dangerous course of action. She'd had that condition for twelve years. Surely people knew her. As she worked her way through the crowd, she would have rendered anyone who touched her ceremonially unclean, including Jesus. Jesus confronted her, but not to scold her. Instead, he said her faith had made her whole.

Myth Buster

Some dismiss miracles as simple misunderstandings by ancient individuals. The healing of lepers puts this idea to rest. Leprosy was a skin disease that included everything from true leprosy to psoriasis. The lesions are very visible. A healing would be obvious to anyone present. Also, a leper was required to appear before the priests to be formally declared healed and allowed to reenter society. Any sign of skin disease would soon be known. The healings were obvious to everyone present. Granted, first-century people did not have the scientific insights we have today, but they were not gullible or stupid.

Final Thought

Leprosy represented sin. In fact, many considered the disease a judgment from God. To the first-century mind, anyone with leprosy brought it on himself. Jesus' willingness to deal with those people reveals that no one is too unclean. Jesus is in the business of making us all clean again.

Check Your Understanding

- **What does Jesus' willingness to touch an untouchable tell us about him?**

It tells us that Jesus has a different set of standards than society. He looks beyond the "disease" and at the person's heart.

- **In some ways, the woman with the blood issue was attempting to "steal" a healing by sneaking up on Jesus, and yet Jesus did not admonish her. In fact, he paid her a compliment. Why?**

Because the woman showed great faith. He also understood the courage it took to face the wrath of the crowd should she have been discovered.

- **If leprosy represents sin, then what do the accounts teach us?**

Jesus can remove our sin as quickly and thoroughly as he removed the leprosy.

Working with Society's Outsiders—
Adulterers, Prostitutes, Outcasts

Jesus crossed the spectrum of society. He spoke with those in the upper ranks and spent time with society's outsiders. Not only did Jesus touch the untouchable, he spent time with the immoral. Seems odd that a man considered a rabbi, a spiritual leader, and a man of God would find no shame numbering among his friends those whom society cast off. Jesus came to change lives, not throw them away. Society drew a circle to keep some people out; Jesus drew a wider circle to keep people in.

✳

John 4:4–30 tells a fascinating story that reveals a great deal about Jesus' view of society's outsiders. Just as certain diseases pushed people out of their communities, so could behavior. Jesus was traveling south and passed through Samaria. The significance is easy to overlook without an understanding of the history of the area. As a rule, Jews avoided Samaria. The region rested between Galilee in the north and Judea in the south. Someone traveling from a town in Galilee to Jerusalem in Judea would normally cross over the Jordan River, travel south, then cross the Jordan River again. All to avoid stepping foot on Samaritan soil.

Come to Me, all you who labor and are heavy laden, and I will give you rest.

Matthew 11:28 NKJV

All that the Father gives me will come to me, and whoever comes to me I will never drive away.

John 6:37 NIV

Why the bigotry? Jews considered Samaritans half-breeds—part Jew, part Gentile. Centuries before, the land had been captured by the Assyrians. Ancient cultures, upon capturing a foreign land, often exported many of the inhabitants and replaced them with people from other conquered regions. In this case, Jews in the area intermarried with Gentiles. Many Jews of the day couldn't overlook the history. Additionally, there remained bad blood over the Samaritans' opposition in rebuilding Jerusalem. Centuries later, animosity remained.

Jesus decided to travel through the country rather than avoid it. While there, he stopped to rest at a well while the disciples went to buy food. He waited in the hot, noonday sun when a woman approached to draw water. There's a clue in that detail. Women normally drew water from wells in the cool of the evening, almost never in the heat of midday. Why was this woman drawing water at that time? It was because of her immoral background. She was not welcome at the well with the other women. She had to come when they weren't around.

Something else happened. As she approached, Jesus asked her for a drink. Sounds innocent enough in our time, but in Jesus' day it was scandalous. First, Jewish men didn't speak directly to women outside their family, and they certainly didn't do so without others around. Second, Jews of any gender seldom spoke to Samaritans, something the woman recognized. Jesus used the situation to engage the woman in a talk about spiritual matters that led to Jesus' admitting to being the Messiah.

Jesus then added a twist. He suggested the woman get her husband. She said she didn't have one. Jesus called her on it. "You are right in saying, 'I have no husband'; for you have had five husbands, and the one you have now is not your husband" (John 4:17–18 NRSV). Jesus was not only speaking to a woman and a Samaritan, but he was also having a public dialogue with an adulterer. The dialogue changed her behavior and her life.

On other occasions Jesus spent time with people his society called sinners. The term *sinner* was applied to a wide range of people, from tax collectors to prostitutes. Observers were quick to criticize, but Jesus gave no indication that he cared. In each case, he cared little about the person's past. He cared about redeeming their lives and souls and about giving them new hope and opportunity.

In the home of Simon the Pharisee (a religious leader), while Jesus reclined at supper, a notorious woman came into the house and washed

Jesus' feet with her tears and hair. Simon was not pleased, and he thought less of Jesus because he allowed it. Jesus told a short story about two men who owed money to a lender. One owed ten times as much as the other. The lender forgave both men their entire debt. Jesus asked which of the two men would love the lender more. Simon gave the obvious answer: the one who owed the most.

> Jesus heard them and answered, "Healthy people don't need a doctor, but sick people do."
>
> Matthew 9:12 CEV

So it was with the woman. She had great sin, so forgiveness would mean more to her than to Simon. Jesus forgave her sins and said she could go in peace.

Something to Ponder

These two women were social outcasts, considered sinners unworthy of the time and effort to give them a chance to change. Often this reinforces the negative behavior. The Bible is clear about each of us bearing the burden of our own sins, but it is also clear that those sins can be forgiven. The past does not have to dictate the future. Jesus is the Savior of the second chance, always ready to accept everyone who comes to him. Jesus refused to accept society's definition of who a worthwhile human being is. To him, everyone deserves an opportunity to change.

Final Thought

 Two social outcasts met the one person who would not mock them. Differences were put aside, and a door of forgiveness and hope was opened. That was then, but what about now? Nothing has changed. Everyone we see has failings, including the person in the mirror.

Check Your Understanding

- **In dealing with the Samaritan woman, Jesus committed several social taboos. Why would he risk the ridicule?**

Jesus valued the woman more than the opinions of others. The fact that she was a Samaritan and a woman did not diminish her in his eyes. She needed the change he could bring.

- **At Simon the Pharisee's house, the division existing between the sinful woman and the religious leader became apparent. What lesson does Simon's attitude teach us?**

Simon's religion was more concerned with appearance than helping others find the change they needed.

- **There are no recorded words from the woman who washed Jesus' feet, yet we know she was repentant. How?**

The woman's tears and humbling actions showed her repentance and desire to be forgiven. She wanted to leave her past behind.

Erasing the Lines of Prejudice

The comedian/actor W. C. Fields quipped, "I am free of all prejudices. I hate everyone equally." The line was meant to garner a laugh, but history has taught us that prejudice has been a disease that humans have struggled with from the beginning. Prejudice has tainted every culture, every nation, and every people group. Usually when we hear the term we think of racial hatred, but prejudice has more colors than that. Jesus dealt with prejudice throughout his entire ministry and took a high road that we all can follow.

The Bible is an honest, untouched revelation. It doesn't candy-coat the accounts. It lays bare the reality of the day, and one ugly reality clearly seen in its pages is the bigotry that permeated every fiber of society. A common Jewish prayer of the day was, "Thank you, God, that I am not a Gentile, a Samaritan, or a woman."

There were several prominent lines of prejudice. First was racial bigotry, an affliction that affected people from every background. Jews generally despised Gentiles and held a special hatred for racially mixed Samaritans. Jews often refused to step on Samaritan soil and shook the dust from their sandals if they did. The feelings were returned with equal loathing. The Jews also despised the Romans who occupied their land. Their hatred was eclipsed only by the level of repugnance the Romans held for the Jews.

The body is a unit, though it is made up of many parts; and though all its parts are many, they form one body. So it is with Christ.

1 Corinthians 12:12 NIV

It's exactly the same no matter what a person's religious background may be: the same God for all of us, acting the same incredibly generous way to everyone who calls out for help.

Romans 10:12 MSG

Religious matters were also a cause for separation. The religious community was divided into groups of priests, Pharisees, Sadducees, Essenes, and others.

Gender was another dividing line. Although some women had businesses and owned property, most women were relegated to a lower level of value. They were vital to the community but remained second-class citizens.

How did Jesus deal with prejudices? He dealt with them by not participating in them. A survey of his miracles shows that Jesus helped Jews, Romans, Gentiles, and women equally. He spoke with the religious conservatives and liberals. Jesus maintained an all-encompassing view that drew every willing believer in, no matter the gender or background.

Take It to Heart

 The key to ending prejudice is to stop seeing differences and begin seeing commonality. Jesus didn't distinguish between Jew and Gentile, male and female. In his eyes, everyone had the same need—a need he came to meet. He changed his culture by not letting his culture change him.

Check Your Understanding

- **Prejudice is often passed from one generation to another without being challenged. Why didn't Jesus adopt the same thinking as his peers?**

Jesus didn't come to be changed, but to change others. He knows that people laugh and cry the same. Old prejudices have no place in his thinking.

- **Bigotry has always plagued humankind. How has Jesus' teaching made inroads into ending prejudice?**

The only way to change prejudice is to change people, and Jesus' message does exactly that.

Jesus Shows Compassion for the Conquerors

No people like to be oppressed. The history of the Jews is one of freedom followed by captivity followed by freedom followed by captivity and, in Jesus' day, an occupying nation. Seeing the disdain the Jews held for the Romans is understandable. Dealing with the Romans was done only on a need-to basis. While some groups warmed to the occupation, most Jews hated the Romans. Insurrections were not uncommon. Jesus lived and worked in those conditions, and he showed mercy to a centurion, a Roman leader in need.

✳

A stroll down any street in Israel would reveal a Roman presence. Seeing a Roman official walking with his wife or servants was common. Even more common was the sight of Roman military. Jesus encountered one such military man in Capernaum. The unnamed man was a centurion, meaning he had command of one hundred soldiers. Unlike most men in his position, he was known for showing kindness to the Jews.

We get another insight into the man when it's revealed that he had a servant close to death, a servant he cared for. Desperate, the Roman military man sent for the Jewish teacher. The two couldn't have been more different. It's doubtful the centurion would have given Jesus a second thought had not his servant teetered on the brink of death.

Since God chose you to be the holy people he loves, you must clothe yourselves with tenderhearted mercy, kindness, humility, gentleness, and patience.

Colossians 3:12 NLT

All of you, have unity of spirit, sympathy, love for one another, a tender heart, and a humble mind. Do not repay evil for evil or abuse for abuse; but, on the contrary, repay with a blessing. It is for this that you were called—that you might inherit a blessing.

1 Peter 3:8–9 NRSV

The people who went to retrieve Jesus made the request in public. What would Jesus do? Granted, the man was kinder to Jews than most, but he was the commander of a large number of soldiers occupying the land. Jesus didn't hesitate. He offered to go and heal the servant. The centurion hesitated and said he was not worthy to have Jesus come under his roof, and then he encouraged Jesus to heal the servant at a distance. Jesus' response? "Truly I say to you, I have not found such great faith with anyone in Israel" (Matthew 8:10 NASB).

Jesus' compassion knew no boundaries. The man had a need, the man had faith, and Jesus was willing to heal. He gave no heed to what others might think.

Final Thought

 Events can reduce us to our basics; basics shared by every human regardless of upbringing. Jesus showed compassion for one of the conquerors by healing his servant. We may not be able to heal, but we can be helpful where we are and show the love of Jesus in the process.

Check Your Understanding

- Why would a pagan-trained Roman military man seek help from Jesus, an itinerant Jewish teacher?

Desperation may have been the motivation. Jesus' reputation preceded him. The centurion had to cross the line that divided conqueror from conquered in order to seek help.

- Word that Jesus helped the Roman would spread quickly and some would certainly be offended, and yet Jesus didn't hesitate. Why?

Jesus was moved by the need of the person, not the history. If Jesus had refused to help, nothing would have changed. The Romans would still have occupied the land. Jesus looked past all that.

Breaking Social Rules

In the 1970s, it was popular to portray Jesus as a rebel, a revolutionary bent on changing the world. The image isn't far wrong. Jesus was not a social rebel, but he did refuse to bend to social pressure. We have already seen cases where Jesus went against social custom. He touched lepers, called a tax collector as a disciple, allowed an adulterous woman to wash his feet, spoke to the Samaritan woman, and healed a Roman's servant. In each of these cases, he had a greater good in mind, a spiritual teaching meant to last through the ages.

✳

Jesus ministered in socially restricted times. Most of Jesus' contact was with Jews who either accepted or rejected him. Over many years, a large set of traditions had been added to Jewish life. These customs were additions to the law of Moses given centuries before. Over time, the traditions took on the weight of law, and breaking tradition would bring heavy criticism.

The Son of Man came eating and drinking, and they say, "Look, a glutton and a winebibber, a friend of tax collectors and sinners!" But wisdom is justified by her children.

Matthew 11:19 NKJV

Everyone who saw this started grumbling, "This man Zacchaeus is a sinner! And Jesus is going home to eat with him."

Luke 19:7 CEV

Mark 7:1-13 tells of a confrontation between Jesus and the Pharisees. Jesus' disciples were eating with "unwashed hands" (v. 2 NKJV). The criticism sounds strange to us today, but it was a serious accusation then. In fact, some considered eating with hands not ceremonially washed equivalent to sexual sin.

The problem rested in superstition and bigotry. One superstition was that demons rested on the hands, and to eat without first undergoing the ritual washing was courting possession. The bigger problem rested in the fear of being rendered unclean by inadvertently touching a Gentile in the marketplace and becoming contaminated. The solution was an elaborate washing ritual with water poured from a pure vessel and rinsing up to the elbows.

Jesus rejected the criticism. He quoted a passage from Isaiah 29:13 and called the critics hypocrites. "You have let go of the commands of God and are holding on to the traditions of men" (Mark 7:8 NIV). Strong words that struck at the heart of the problem.

Another round of accusations came when the same group of people witnessed the disciples plucking heads of grain and eating them (Matthew 12:1–8). Not a bad thing to do most days, but this was the Sabbath and work on the Sabbath was forbidden. Again, an accusation of religious unlawfulness was leveled at Jesus. Jesus responded with his favorite tactic: calling to mind Scripture. He reminded them of a time when King David ate bread dedicated to priests and how the priests work on the Sabbath but are not guilty. He then made a statement sure to upset them: "For the Son of Man is Lord of the Sabbath" (v. 8 NKJV).

This led to yet another confrontation, this time a setup meant to entrap Jesus. Matthew 12:9–14 tells us that Jesus traveled to a synagogue where a man with a withered hand waited. They asked Jesus if it was lawful to heal on the Sabbath. Jesus answered with subtle action. He told the man to stretch out his hand. A moment later it was healed. It's interesting that Jesus took no physical action that could be construed as work. As far as we know he made no movement at all, and yet his accusers were so angry they plotted to kill him. Odd response. A man underwent a remarkable and very visible healing, and the enemies of Jesus were upset because it happened on the Sabbath.

Another common complaint was Jesus' unapologetic contact with tax collectors and sinners. In Luke 5:30 the term *sinner* most likely refers to unobservant Jews, those who didn't follow the model set before them. They were people others refused to associate with, and yet Jesus found them comfortable company. Jesus' response was to restate his purpose: "Those who are well have no need of a physician, but those who are sick. I have not come to call the righteous, but sinners, to repentance" (Luke 5:31–32 NKJV).

Jesus had women followers. Today that comment has no shock value, but it did in Jesus' day. Some think he may have had a circle of female disciples. We can't say with certainty, but we do know women played an important role in his ministry. Matthew 27:55 mentions women who followed from Galilee to Jerusalem to "care for his needs" (NIV). Mark 15:40 mentions several women by name: Mary Magdalene, Mary the mother of James, and Salome. Luke 8:3 adds Joanna and Susanna. According to Mark 15:41, "There were many other women who had come up with him to Jerusalem" (NRSV).

> These are the "grumpers," the bellyachers, grabbing for the biggest piece of the pie, talking big, saying anything they think will get them ahead.
>
> Jude 16 MSG

Myth Buster

One woman to follow Jesus was Mary Magdalene. It's become popular to link her romantically with Jesus, going so far as to say they married and had children. Such speculation has no basis in history or grounding in the Bible. There is no evidence to think that Mary Magdalene was anything more than a faithful follower and supporter. Another myth associated with Mary Magdalene states she was a prostitute. This comes from confusing her with the woman who anointed Jesus' feet with perfume (Luke 7:36–39). There is no biblical reason to believe that Mary Magdalene was a prostitute.

Final Thought

 Jesus' mission would allow nothing to stand in the way He excmplified the obedient life, but his obedience was to God and his mission, not to social contrivances. If we worry too much about what is happening around us, we will take our eyes off what lies ahead.

Check Your Understanding

- The thing that upset Jesus' enemies the most was unwillingness to comply with the same religious rules they did. Wouldn't it have been easier if he had just gone along?

It would have been much easier, but it would have also diminished his ministry. The people needed to see that Jesus was not interested in obedience to traditions; he was interested in obedience to God.

- Jesus' detractors considered him a Sabbath breaker, but was he really?

No. Jesus put a proper definition on the Sabbath. He stated the Sabbath was designed for people and not the other way around.

- Jesus made it clear that he didn't care if he broke social rules dealing with association by spending time with undesirables. Why didn't he care?

Those people were at the heart of his mission. He spent time with them because they needed him most.

The Meaning of Miracles

The most noticeable aspect of the Gospels is their record of Jesus' miracles. Between them, they record thirty-five supernatural events. Matthew records twenty miracles, Mark eighteen, Luke twenty, and John seven. The miracles have a purpose. To some they might seem like magic tricks performed to gather attention, but they were much more. Certainly, miracles caused word of Jesus to spread quickly. It drew crowds filled with needy people wanting a miracle of their own. Who can blame them? Miracles had a function.

✻

M iracles are supernatural events that achieve some meaningful purpose. *Supernatural* means "above nature" and refers to something that is beyond the norm. Often someone will say, "But miracles are impossible." That, of course, is the point. Yes, they're impossible; they break the laws of physics, of space, and even of time. The word *miracle* means "wonder." A miracle stops us in our tracks. It makes us question our vision and maybe even our sanity. The Bible writers used different terms to describe a miracle, including such terms as *powers, signs, works*, and *wonders*.

A miracle is the impossible happening before the eyes of witnesses. It

That message spread throughout Judea, beginning in Galilee after the baptism that John announced: how God anointed Jesus of Nazareth with the Holy Spirit and with power; how he went about doing good and healing all who were oppressed by the devil, for God was with him.

Acts 10:37–38 NRSV

God himself showed that his message was true by working all kinds of powerful miracles and wonders. He also gave his Holy Spirit to anyone he chose to

Hebrews 2:4 CEV

is an event made to happen by the miracle worker. Jesus never asked permission to do miracles; he just did them. Nonetheless, his miracles were not haphazard. Each miracle did two things. First, it met a pressing need. Second, it revealed something about Jesus.

We've examined a few miracles already. For example, the woman with the blood issue was healed by touching Jesus' garment (Luke 8:43–48). We shouldn't think that Jesus was unaware of her. It's interesting that she was healed without Jesus' saying a word or even facing her. The pressing need was this woman's twelve-year struggle with the disease and the fact she was considered unclean, not to be touched. What does this story reveal about Jesus? That his love extends to the fringes of society, that his love touches the untouchable. It also shows his power over physical affliction.

There are thirty-five recorded miracles worked by Jesus, but he did many more. John wrote in his Gospel that "there are also many other things which Jesus did" (21:25 NASB). We have no idea how many miracles he worked during his three-year ministry. No doubt, he did some that very few, if any, knew about.

Miracles give credence to Jesus' teaching and proclamations. Jesus was not the first person to claim to be the Christ, nor was he the last one. Acts 5:36 mentions a man named Theudas who was "claiming to be somebody" (NIV) and gathered about four hundred followers before being killed. Nothing came of his movement. Jesus warned that people would follow claiming to be the Christ. They were to be avoided. Jesus claimed to be the Son of God, equal with God, and the Messiah, and he backed his words with miracles.

Peter mentioned the miracles in his first sermon: "Men of Israel, listen to this: Jesus of Nazareth was a man accredited by God to you by miracles, wonders and signs, which God did among you through him, as you yourselves know" (Acts 2:22 NIV). Peter used three words to describe the supernatural events Jesus worked. The first is *miracle,* which translates the Greek word *dunamis.* Originally the word meant "force, power, ability." We get the English word *dynamite* from it. *Wonder* speaks to the viewers' response. The observer wonders how such a thing could be. *Signs* refer to the miracle's ability to verify Jesus' claims about himself.

Anyone could make the claims Jesus made, but only Jesus backed up his claims with miracles that no one else could do.

The next Sabbath he taught in the Jewish meeting place. Many of the people who heard him were amazed and asked, "How can he do all this? Where did he get such wisdom and the power to work these miracles?"

Mark 6:2 CEV

Peter told the congregation (the same people who called for Jesus' execution) that the miracles "accredited" Jesus. The miracles proved the claim.

Miracles made Jesus' ministry noticeable, unforgettable, and believable. The wide range and variety of miracles worked by Jesus lent credence to his claims. Healing the lame and the blind, stopping storms in a moment, and raising the dead are all beyond the powers and skills of the best showman. Jesus' miracles have stood the test of time.

Myth Buster

Miracles are hard to believe, and they should be. Many dismiss miracles, assuming believers are gullible. We do not suspend our intellect to believe. Many intelligent people believe in the miracles of Jesus. These are people with advanced education in areas such as engineering, the sciences, psychology, and medicine. Ignorance is not a requirement to believe in miracles; intelligence is.

Jesus healed a blind man who later endured a cross-examination by Jesus' enemies. Frustrated, the man said, "I don't know whether he is a sinner, but I know this: I was blind, and now I can see!" (John 9:25 NLT).

Final Thought

Billy Graham said, "At strategic moments God again and again manifested himself to men by miracles so they had outward, confirming evidence that the words they heard from God's servants were true." This is true for Jesus' miracles. They were strategic and verified that he was the Son of God.

Check Your Understanding

- **The miracles Jesus worked had a purpose in the first century. Do those same miracles have the same purpose today?**

Yes. As then, they authenticate the message of Jesus. The difference is that we're not eyewitnesses to those works. Nonetheless, we have very reliable sources.

- **Were confirming miracles like those Jesus worked an everyday occurrence?**

No. Since we are able to read the accounts over a short period, we often think that one miracle followed another. Jesus' miracles happened over a three-year period. The era of miracles carried on through the ministry of the apostles.

- **What difference does it make that many people are skeptical about miracles?**

No difference. Skepticism is natural, but denying an event doesn't make the event untrue.

Types of Miracles

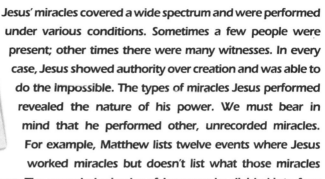

Jesus' miracles covered a wide spectrum and were performed under various conditions. Sometimes a few people were present; other times there were many witnesses. In every case, Jesus showed authority over creation and was able to do the impossible. The types of miracles Jesus performed revealed the nature of his power. We must bear in mind that he performed other, unrecorded miracles. For example, Matthew lists twelve events where Jesus worked miracles but doesn't list what those miracles were. The recorded miracles of Jesus can be divided into four groups: power over nature, healings, exorcisms, and resurrections.

Nine times Jesus showed power over nature. The first of these was turning water into wine. Others include a miraculous catch of fish (Luke 5:1-11), a miracle repeated after the resurrection (John 21:1-11). Jesus stilled a storm (Luke 8:22-25), multiplied a small bit of bread to feed more than five thousand people (Mark 6:34-44) one time and four thousand another time (Mark 8:1-9). When pressed for the temple tax, Jesus sent Peter fishing where he caught a fish with the tax coin in its mouth (Matthew 17:24-27), and he cursed a fig tree that died immediately (Matthew 21:18-19).

He went all over Galilee. He used synagogue for meeting places and taught people the truth of God. God's kingdom was his theme—that beginning right now they were under God's government, a good government! He also healed people of their diseases and of the bad effects of their bad lives.

Matthew 4:23 MSG

Most of the miracles were healings. Seventeen such acts are recorded and cover disorders such as blindness (Matthew 9:27-31), physical handicaps like a withered hand (Matthew 12:9-13), paralysis (Matthew 9:2-8), deafness (Mark 7:31-37), leprosy (Matthew 8:2-4), and bleeding (Luke 8:43–48). And in each case, the healing was immediate and permanent.

Six times Jesus performed exorcisms. These dramatic events show Jesus' authority over the spiritual realm. In several cases, the demons spoke (Matthew 8:28–34; Mark 1:23–28). Sometimes the demon activity was associated with physical illness, making the healing a twofold blessing (Matthew 9:32–33).

Jesus performed three resurrections. The first was the raising of the widow's son in the town of Nain. This happened as the funeral procession was under way (Luke 7:11–15). In the second case, Jesus brought Jairus's daughter back to life after her sudden death (Matthew 9:18, 23–25). The most famous resurrection was that of Lazarus in Bethany, the place where Jesus wept (John 11:17–44).

Final Thought

 There is no way to know how many miracles Jesus performed, but it's safe to say that they numbered in the hundreds if not the thousands. The miracles demonstrated Jesus' authority over nature, over biology, over the unseen spiritual realm, and even over death.

Check Your Understanding

- **Why do you suppose there was such a wide variety of miracles?**

The miracles covered every area of life's needs, from food, to health, to death, and showed that Jesus is Lord of all things.

- **Miracles are very personal things, even when the miracle touches the lives of thousands. Why the personal touch rather than some dramatic display like causing the stars to rearrange in the night sky?**

The motive behind the miracles was not just to authenticate his message but to provide some useful benefit. Jesus didn't show off; he met needs.

The First Miracle

First events, first words, first actions often set the tone for everything that follows. The first words of a speech dictate the tone; the first few plays of a football game establish how the contest will be played. A short time before Jesus began his public ministry, he was called upon to do something about an impossible situation. To meet the need, Jesus performed his first earthly miracle. The way he conducted that miracle set the tone for his entire ministry and showed Jesus' powerful and unique approach to his work. The story is told in John 2:1–11.

Jesus' first miracle took place in the village of Cana in the northern region of Palestine called Galilee. Little is known about the town, and it has long since gone out of existence. Many scholars think it was located eight miles north of Nazareth.

Jesus, his mother, Mary, and four of his disciples attended a wedding. Modern weddings differ greatly from first-century Jewish weddings. Our weddings usually consist of a marriage ceremony followed by a reception. Together the two events run from two hours to six or more hours. In Jesus' day, a wedding lasted *seven days* with the whole community invited.

> Anyone who belongs to Christ is a new person. The past is forgotten, and everything is new. God has done it all!
>
> 2 Corinthians 5:17–18 CEV
>
> God, make a fresh start in me, shape a Genesis week from the chaos of my life.
>
> Psalm 51:10 MSG

Mary was somehow deeply involved in the proceedings. To be a good host to so many people required help. Mary was one such helper. Why? No one is certain. There is good reason to believe that she may have been related to the family in charge of the wedding. In a time when families kept close ties, it would have been normal to call upon cousins, aunts, uncles, brothers, and sisters to help. Whatever the relationship, Mary took an active role in the celebration—and then social disaster struck.

They ran out of wine.

Two factors here: First, to the first-century Middle Easterner, hospitality was paramount—people judged others by their kindness. Second, there were no grocery stores to replenish supplies quickly.

Perhaps fearing the family would suffer a haunting social embarrassment, Mary informed Jesus of the problem. His response has puzzled many: "Woman, what does that have to do with us? My hour has not yet come" (John 2:4 NASB). Was Jesus being rude? No, and here's why.

Some balk at Jesus' use of "Woman." To address one's mother that way today might draw an unwanted response. In Jesus' day, the term was one of honor. Jesus used the term six times, including during the horrible hours on the cross where he said, "Woman, behold, your son!" (John 19:26 NASB).

Jesus reminded her that the starting time for his public ministry had not arrived. She responded as only a mother could. She turned to the servants and said, "Whatever He says to you, do it" (John 2:5 NASB). That seemed to settle the matter.

The only visible act Jesus did was to give instructions to the servants. Those instructions were to (1) bring in the water pots, (2) fill them to the brim with water, and (3) take a sample to the wine steward. Jesus lifted nothing; touched nothing.

The steward declared it the best wine of the celebration. Usually the better wine was served first and the lesser wine later. This was a reversal of a long-held practice.

To understand this miracle we need to understand an ancient custom. The stone water pots Jesus called for were never meant to hold wine. The fact that he called for these pots instead of using the empty wine containers and skins is revealing. Water pots were kept outside the house and were used for ceremonial washing. Every Jew practiced a hand-washing ritual that required cleaning one's hands and forearms.

Not to do so was a breach of social etiquette. People of the day believed they could be defiled by eating and drinking with unwashed hands.

The pots were of different sizes. The passage tells us they held between twenty and thirty gallons. The fact that they had to be filled again meant there were enough people to have nearly emptied them merely by washing their hands.

We are God's masterpiece. He has created us anew in Christ Jesus, so that we can do the good things he planned for us long ago.

Ephesians 2:10 NLT

Jesus ordered the pots filled to the brim, indicating that nothing could be added to them. No one, neither Jesus nor his disciples, could add wine or anything else to the fluid without the containers overflowing.

Without lifting a finger, the water turned to wine. An impossibility, but then that's why we call it a miracle.

Digging Deeper

To understand the miracle we must see the message. Jesus preached a sermon without words. First, the containers. There were six of them. When the Bible mentions a specific number, it is always good to ask why. Biblical numbers represent unstated concepts: three refers to deity, seven to perfection, and forty to testing. Six represents humankind. The six stone pots represent humanity filled with the "dirt" of sin.

When Jesus changed the water to wine, he converted the dirty to the clean, and that sums up Jesus' ministry and sacrifice: turning sinful people into something new and complete.

Final Thought

Wine is the product of fruit that is allowed to ferment, a process that requires at least fourteen days. Four hundred compounds give wine its unique look, taste, and color. Water has none of that, and yet Jesus turned the nothing into something.

Jesus changes his followers in unimaginable ways.

Check Your Understanding

- **This is one of the few miracles worked in steps. Why do you suppose Jesus chose to work in such a fashion?**

The systematic approach allowed others to be involved.

- **Jesus didn't touch the pots or the water. Why?**

By keeping his distance, only the four disciples present, the servants, and Mary would know how the wine came to be.

- **To the ancient Jewish mind, wine represented joy (Psalm 104:15). Does that have bearing on the miracle?**

Yes. New life in Jesus is a joyous thing.

- **Based on Mary's approach in asking Jesus to deal with the lack of wine, do you think Jesus worked miracles before this event?**

There is no way to know. Tradition says he did, but there is no evidence of it in the Bible. Still, it seems Mary knew of his ability to solve the problem.

Miracles over Disease

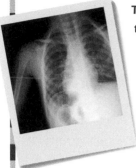

The human body is an amazing machine with 206 bones that support and protect our internal organs. Six chemicals make up the body: oxygen, carbon, hydrogen, nitrogen, calcium, and phosphorus. These elements combine to make everything from the hundred billion cells in our brains to the thirty-seven hundred miles of blood vessels that feed the hundreds of millions of cells that make us, us. Amazing as the body is, it is subject to disease and damage. It was no different in Jesus' day. Illness was present. Lack of advanced medical care made simple illnesses dangerous. Jesus cured scores of diseases.

Most of Jesus' recorded miracles involved the curing of physical ailments. In most cases the disorder was described, but in two cases the illnesses remained unknown. In those situations, the sick individual was not present and Jesus healed them without ever seeing them. One was a nobleman's son who lay at home dying. Jesus promised the boy would be healed, and the nobleman received the good news as he returned home. The second unknown disease was the one that affected the centurion's servant. Again, the servant was not in the presence of Jesus, yet he was healed.

Twice Jesus healed paralytics. The extent of the paralysis could be seen in their dependence on others. Jesus visited a pool of Bethesda that many believed had curative powers (John 5:3-4). Jesus asked what appears to be a ridiculous question: "Do

At that very time Jesus cured many who had diseases, sicknesses and evil spirits, and gave sight to many who were blind. So he replied to the messengers, "Go back and report to John what you have seen and heard: The blind receive sight, the lame walk, those who have leprosy are cured, the deaf hear, the dead are raised, and the good news is preached to the poor."

Luke 7:21–22 NIV

you want to get well?" (v. 6 NIV). Most likely Jesus asked the question to get the man's attention. Jesus told him to stand and walk. The man was immediately healed. The second occurrence was an event we discussed earlier. Four men brought their paralyzed friend to Jesus but couldn't get close because of the crowds. They tore through the roof and lowered their companion to Jesus. The man walked on his own from the house.

An account in Matthew 8:14-15 reveals a healing done for one of his disciples. Visiting Peter's home, Jesus and the disciples discovered that Peter's mother-in-law was ill with a fever. Jesus took her by the hand, and she arose healed and well enough to prepare food.

There are two accounts of deformities made right. The first we touched on in an earlier chapter. A man with a withered hand was healed (Matthew 12:9-13). Whatever the cause, it was noticeable and well known. It must have been amazing to see the arm become whole again. The next defor-

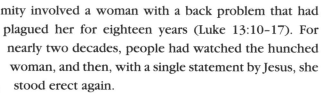

mity involved a woman with a back problem that had plagued her for eighteen years (Luke 13:10-17). For nearly two decades, people had watched the hunched woman, and then, with a single statement by Jesus, she stood erect again.

Twice Jesus healed lepers. Once he healed an individual, and once he healed a group of ten. Matthew 8:2-4, as we saw earlier, reports how a leper approached Jesus and asked to be healed. Jesus did what no one else would have done—he touched the man. The moment he did, the leper was made well. In the second encounter, a group of lepers called to Jesus for help. Ten of them had pinned their hopes on Jesus. Unwilling to approach, they shouted their request from a distance. Jesus responded in like fashion, telling them to go to the priests to be declared clean. All were healed, but only one came back to say thank you.

Four of the seventeen healing miracles dealt with the blind. Jesus' technique varied with these men. In Matthew 9:27-31, Jesus healed two blind men by touching their eyes. With the blind man at Bethsaida (Mark 8:22-26), Jesus led him out of the village and spit on his eyes. Jesus repeated the process, making this the only incremental miracle. In the third case, Jesus made mud from spittle and dirt, applied it to the man's eyes, and sent him to wash in the pool of Siloam (John 9:1-7). This miracle was different from the others because the man had been born blind. In the healing of blind Bartimaeus (Mark 10:46-52), Jesus healed by simple command.

As He was now drawing near the descent of the Mount of Olives, the whole multitude of the disciples began to rejoice and praise God with a loud voice for all the mighty works they had seen, saying: "Blessed is the King who comes in the name of the LORD! Peace in heaven and glory in the highest!"

Luke 19.37-38 NKJV

Jesus also healed deafness (Mark 7:31-37), edema once (Luke 14:1-6), and bleeding once (Luke 8:43-48). During Jesus' arrest, Peter struck a man with a sword who had come to seize Jesus and severed his ear (Luke 22:49-51). Jesus miraculously reattached the ear and then submitted to the arrest.

Those who choose not to believe in miracles often dismiss these healings by attributing them to trickery, but a careful examination of the events puts that argument to rest. Jesus' healing miracles have several things in common. First, they were always performed in front of witnesses, sometimes many witnesses. Also, the miracles were worked on individuals with well-known and long-lasting illnesses. Some of the beneficiaries had lived with their problems for many years. Everyone who knew them knew the afflictions were real. The drastic change caused by the healing could easily be verified.

Final Thought

Jesus was able to help others in ways we cannot, but our attitude should be the same as his. Jesus didn't heal everyone at one time; he healed them as he encountered them. We can make a difference by doing what we can where we are.

Check Your Understanding

■ **Knowing Jesus performed scores or hundreds of other miracles, why do you think the Gospel writers selected the ones they did?**

The miracles we have in the Gospels are representative of Jesus' ministry. There are forms of spiritual blindness, paralysis, death, and the like. The Gospel writers included those miracles that highlighted Jesus' message.

■ **Are there more to the miracles than it at first seems?**

Every healing carried an unspoken sermon with it. Touching the leper showed that no matter how "unclean" we are, Jesus will accept us. Raising the dead reminds us that a spiritually dead person can be brought back to life.

■ **Did Jesus heal just to get attention?**

No, several times he instructed the healed not to tell anyone. All of these were personal.

■ **In some ways, healing proved counterproductive. Why?**

Jesus suffered from a crowd-control problem. The more he healed, the more the crowds grew. At times, it was almost impossible for Jesus to move.

■ **What do healings prove?**

That Jesus had power over the physical universe, including the intricacies and complexities of the human body. To heal in an instant could be achieved only by the power of God.

Miracles Done over Distance

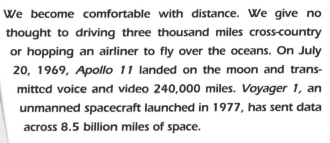

We become comfortable with distance. We give no thought to driving three thousand miles cross-country or hopping an airliner to fly over the oceans. On July 20, 1969, *Apollo 11* landed on the moon and transmitted voice and video 240,000 miles. *Voyager 1*, an unmanned spacecraft launched in 1977, has sent data across 8.5 billion miles of space.

Things were different in Jesus' day. Travel was limited to foot or animal. News traveled at the speed of walking. Distance mattered then. For Jesus distance was no obstacle, something he proved by performing a miracle without being at the scene.

Jesus returned to Cana, the town where he turned water into wine, and was immediately met by a man whose son lay dying twenty-five miles away in Capernaum (John 4:46-53). We don't know his exact position, only that John called him a nobleman. The man had power and prestige, neither of which could help his son. He did what desperate fathers do: reach for any strand of hope. He begged Jesus to come and heal his son, but Jesus refused to go. Instead, Jesus told the nobleman to go home and his son would live. The nobleman did the incredible— he took Jesus at his word. On his way home a servant found him and

> Call for help when you're in trouble—I'll help you, and you'll honor me.
>
> Psalm 50:15 MSG
>
> I was terrified and thought, "They've chased me far away from you!" But you answered my prayer when I shouted for help.
>
> Psalm 31:22 CEV

delivered the good news about the boy's sudden recovery. The nobleman asked what time the turnaround took place, and the time matched Jesus' proclamation.

Matthew 8:5-13 tells a similar story with some reversals. Jesus entered Capernaum and a centurion met him. A centurion was a military leader in charge of one hundred soldiers. The centurion's servant was deathly ill, and the military man pleaded for Jesus to heal him. Jesus offered to go to the man's house, but the centurion said he was unworthy to have Jesus in his home. He stated his belief that Jesus could heal the servant without going to the house. Jesus did just that.

Time and space could not confine the power of Jesus to work miracles. No person was beyond his reach.

Final Thought

Two men, each with similar needs, approached Jesus and asked for help. He didn't ask questions. He didn't need information; he wanted requests made in faith. That hasn't changed. Jesus remains approachable. Jesus didn't heal everyone, but when healing was appropriate, miles of distance couldn't stop him.

Check Your Understanding

- **How did the nobleman show his faith when he asked Jesus to come to his home twenty-five miles away?**

He revealed his faith by taking Jesus at his word. The nobleman had no proof that what Jesus said was true, but he believed it anyway and returned home to his healed son.

- **How did the centurion reveal his faith when he asked Jesus to heal his beloved servant?**

He did so by stating his belief that Jesus could work the miracle even though distance separated him from the one needing his help.

Miracles Involving the Dead

The boxer Joe Lewis quipped, "Everybody wants to go to heaven, but nobody wants to die." It's a keen observation. Common as death is, it is upsetting to see and makes us feel helpless. Illnesses might be cured. Injuries can heal. Death seems so permanent. The Gospels record three times when Jesus upturned the normal course of things and reversed death. His own conquest over death shows the power of God over everything in the human experience. Jesus healed many ill people, and no disease was beyond his power. He also proved that not even death was a match for him.

✳

As Jesus neared the town of Nain, he came upon a funeral procession. Luke 7:11–17 makes two touching observations: the deceased was an only son; and his mother was a widow. Today the time between the death and the funeral can be a week or longer. First-century Jews buried the departed the same day. Less than a day had passed from the time the widow's son died and when the funeral procession began. The procession included a wood stretcher with the deceased resting on it carried by several men. Jesus felt compassion for the woman and did something about it. He stopped the procession and touched the stretcher. Then, in what had to

The blind see and the lame walk; the lepers are cleansed and the deaf hear; the dead are raised up and the poor have the gospel preached to them.

Matthew 11:5 NKJV

I tell you the truth, a time is coming and has now come when the dead will hear the voice of the Son of God and those who hear will live. For as the Father has life in himself, so he has granted the Son to have life in himself.

John 5:25–26 NIV

seem an act of madness, Jesus addressed the young man, telling him to rise. And he did.

Jairus was a synagogue official who sought Jesus for help. His twelve-year-old daughter was close to death (Mark 5:22-24, 35-43). Before Jesus could walk to Jairus's house, a servant found them and reported the man's daughter had died. Jesus and the crowd following him continued to the house where mourners had already gathered. At the girl's deathbed, Jesus took the girl's hand and told her to rise. And she did.

The most famous resurrection took place with Lazarus, Jesus' friend who had died several days before (John 11:17-44) and was buried in the family tomb. Jesus ordered that the stone sealing the tomb's entrance be moved away, and then called for Lazarus to come out. And he did, still bound in burial wrappings.

Final Thought

Jesus stopped a funeral to raise a dead son, and he went to the house and deathbed of a twelve-year-old girl and to the tomb of a man buried days before. In each case, compassion moved him to act. Jesus not only knows our pain—he feels it. We have an emotional Savior.

Check Your Understanding

- **Of the thirty-five recorded miracles, only three show the dead coming back to life. Why so few?**

First, we don't have a complete list of all Jesus' miracles. It is possible he performed other resurrections. Second, death is the natural course of life and is something that won't end until Jesus returns again.

- **It is interesting to note that Jesus raised an only son, an only daughter, and an only brother. Is there some meaning to this?**

In each case, there were circumstances that stirred Jesus' compassion. The variety of persons shows that Jesus cares for young and old, rich and poor, and powerful and helpless.

Miracles over Nature

Of Jesus' thirty-five miracles, nine of them demonstrated his power over nature. Of course, every miracle shows power over nature, but these are distinguished from the miracles of healing, resurrection, and exorcism. Nine times Jesus broke the laws of physics, chemistry, meteorology, and animal behavior. As with all miracles, Jesus performed these acts to prove his deity, to prove his claims, to support his teaching, and to meet the needs of people. Each miracle had a purpose and a message. With each miracle over nature, Jesus showed his authority over creation.

There are many ways to categorize Jesus' miracles over nature. We can say these supernatural acts demonstrated Jesus' authority over the molecular world, over the animal world, and over the larger physical world. Take, for example, Jesus' first miracle: turning water into wine. While we can't say exactly what Jesus did that converted simple H_2O into wine, complete with the necessary sugars and fruit material, we can assume that he did something at the molecular level. Three miracles fit into this category: water to wine (John 2:1-11); feeding the five thousand (Matthew 14:14-21; Mark 6:34-44; Luke 9:12-17; John 6:5-13); and feeding the four thousand (Matthew 15:32-39; Mark 8:1-9). In each case, it appears Jesus performed some supernatural act at the atomic level. In the case of the feeding of the five thousand and the

He told them, "Let your net down on the right side of your boat, and you will catch some fish." They did, and the net was so full of fish that they could not drag it up into the boat.

John 21:6 CEV

When the disciples saw Him walking on the sea, they were troubled, saying, "It is a ghost!" And they cried out for fear. But immediately Jesus spoke to them, saying, "Be of good cheer! It is I; do not be afraid."

Matthew 14:26-27 NKJV

four thousand, a small amount of food—enough for one person—was multiplied to feed thousands. The biblical counts of five thousand and four thousand represent less than the actual number. Only the men were counted. If we assume women and children were present, then those numbers can be tripled.

Some of the most stunning miracles were performed over the larger physical world. Three of the Gospels (Matthew 8:18, 23-27; Mark 4:35-41; Luke 8:22-25) record an incident where Jesus "stilled" a raging storm with a single word. The Sea of Galilee is subject to lake-effect storms, storms that arise suddenly and can turn calm waters into a maelstrom. Stuck in the middle of it were several terrified disciples, men who knew the lake well and had spent many hours on it fishing. The storm came in so quickly and ferociously it terrified hardened fishermen who believed they were about to die. As with all storms, those tempests carry a lot of energy, yet Jesus calmed the storm in moments. We can only guess how many factors he had to change to make this miracle happen.

Perhaps the best-known miracle over the physical world is Jesus' walking on water. This event is so difficult for some to believe they've resorted to nonsensical explanations. Miracles are supposed to be hard to believe and impossible to explain. They wouldn't be miracles otherwise. How did Jesus manage to walk on water? Perhaps Jesus did something on the molecular level there as well. All we know is, in the middle of a storm, Jesus was able to walk on water as if moving over solid ground.

Jesus also cursed a fig tree as an object lesson for the disciples (Matthew 21:18-19; Mark 11:12-14). The tree died almost immediately. Jesus worked this only "destructive" miracle. While it is true the tree died right before the eyes of the disciples, Jesus' purpose was to teach about faith, prayer, and belief.

Jesus also showed power over animals. Interestingly, the only recorded miracles we have of Jesus and animals deal with fish. Twice Jesus told some of his disciples who were fishing from a boat to cast the net on

A fierce storm came up. High waves were breaking into the boat, and it began to fill with water. Jesus was sleeping at the back of the boat with his head on a cushion. The disciples woke him up, shouting, "Teacher, don't you care that we're going to drown?" When Jesus woke up, he rebuked the wind and said to the water, "Silence! Be still!" Suddenly the wind stopped, and there was a great calm. Then he asked them, "Why are you afraid? Do you still have no faith?" The disciples were absolutely terrified. "Who is this man?" they asked each other. "Even the wind and waves obey him!"

Mark 4:37–41 NLT

the other side of the craft (Luke 5:1-11; John 21:1-11). It seems an odd thing to command. Why would fish cluster on, say, the left side of the boat and not the right? In both cases, fish filled the nets to the breaking point. The other fish miracle is odder still. When pressed for the temple tax, Jesus sent Peter fishing. Peter drew in a fish with a coin in its mouth—the precise coin needed to pay the tax (Matthew 17:24-27).

However we classify these miracles, the primary point remains the same: Jesus exhibited power over every aspect of creation. Where we are subject to creation, creation was and is subject to him.

As with all the miracles Jesus performed, each carried a lesson about him, his love, and his teaching, and it met some pressing need. Jesus was not a magician performing tricks to entertain. These miracles had a greater purpose.

Myth Buster

Some have tried to dismiss Jesus' miracles by assuming that the people of Jesus' day were too ignorant to know what was going on. It is a common mistake to think that ancient people were unaware, superstitious, and too uneducated to know when they were being fooled. Ancient people achieved a great many things

and showed ingenuity. The people of Jesus' day were not fools. Feeding five thousand people on a hillside from someone's lunch could not have been trickery, nor could stopping a storm—an event that happened in a moment—have been. Miracles are hard to believe, but not impossible.

Final Thought

 We should never be so amazed by the miracle that we forget the miracle worker. Miracles over the molecular, animal, and physical worlds have a purpose beyond amazing us. Every miracle is meant to direct our eyes to Jesus, to his ministry, and, most of all, to his words.

Check Your Understanding

- **Why do so many people have trouble believing in miracles?**

Miracles are unusual. They are impossible events that are nonetheless true. Our society teaches us to be skeptical, which is good, but we must remember, that which is impossible for us is common for God.

- **Jesus' miracles over nature showed his power over creation. Why was that important?**

Jesus made many claims about himself including the claim that he is the Son of God. Only God has the power to change nature by simple command. By demonstrating his authority over nature, Jesus was showing his deity.

- **In several cases, such as Jesus' walking on the water and stopping the storm, the disciples reacted with fear. Why do you suppose that was?**

By definition, miracles are events that supersede human experience, are unexpected, and are beyond expectation. To witness such power is intimidating.

Miracles with Messages

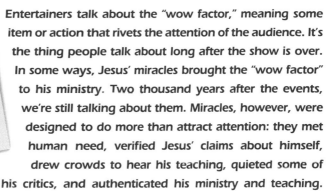

Entertainers talk about the "wow factor," meaning some item or action that rivets the attention of the audience. It's the thing people talk about long after the show is over. In some ways, Jesus' miracles brought the "wow factor" to his ministry. Two thousand years after the events, we're still talking about them. Miracles, however, were designed to do more than attract attention: they met human need, verified Jesus' claims about himself, drew crowds to hear his teaching, quieted some of his critics, and authenticated his ministry and teaching. Miracles did something else as well—they carried a message.

✳

Every miracle has a foundational message. Sometimes the messages are easy to see, others take a little more study. Twice, Jesus fed a multitude (Matthew 14:14–21; 15:32–39). Using the numbers mentioned in the Bible, Jesus fed a group of five thousand men plus women and children; then later did the same for four thousand. A casual reading might lead us to think that Jesus worked the same miracle twice. He did, but there's more to it.

In the first case—the only one of Jesus' thirty-five miracles recorded in all four Gospels—the crowd was so large the disciple Philip estimated that two hundred denarii might not be enough to buy food for everyone. A denarius equaled a day's wages. Philip was suggesting that eight months' wages wouldn't do the job. Andrew brought five fish and two loaves of bread to Jesus— not even enough to feed the disciples. Yet Jesus multiplied the food to

Do you not yet understand, or remember the five loaves of the five thousand and how many baskets you took up? Nor the seven loaves of the four thousand and how many large baskets you took up?

Matthew 16:9–10 NKJV

When you have eaten your fill, be sure to praise the LORD your God for the good land he has given you.

Deuteronomy 8:10 NLT

feed the entire crowd. He did the same with seven loaves and a few fish. In each case, they gathered leftovers: twelve baskets from the five thousand; seven baskets from the four thousand. Since only men were counted in these events, the crowds may have been double, making the miracle all the more impressive. Between the two miracles, it is possible Jesus fed, from a handful of food, more than twenty thousand people.

Like many miracles, these two supernatural events have an underlying meaning. Jesus performed miracles for many reasons, but many times the miracles carried deep lessons. What was the message here? It is found in the numbers. Numbers make these miracles different, not the size of the crowd, but the baskets of leftovers. In the Bible, numbers are often symbolic. For example, the number three represents completeness; six is the number of man; forty is often associated with judgment. Twelve often represents the Hebrews. For example, there were twelve tribes of Israel.

The feeding of the five thousand took place on Jewish soil. When everyone had eaten their fill, the disciples gathered up the remainder. It was enough to fill twelve baskets. The temptation is to dismiss this as mere coincidence, but the next miraculous feeding won't let us, after which seven baskets of leftovers were gathered.

Seven sometimes referred to non-Jews—the Gentiles. Jesus worked the first miracle in Jewish territory; he conducted the second miraculous feeding on Gentile ground, an area settled by seven different Gentile groups fourteen hundred years before. (Deuteronomy 7:1). There was one feeding miracle for the Jews and one for the Gentiles.

The two miracles have many similarities. Both situations began with crowds eager to be near Jesus. Both occurred in the country away from cities. Both stirred up compassion in Jesus. Both involved fish and bread. Both began in doubt but ended in glory. Both involved the disciples' distributing food. Both showed Jesus giving thanks for the food. Both involved the multiplication of a little into a lot. And both had leftovers that were gathered by the disciples.

There were also remarkable differences. The number fed was five thousand men in the first case, four thousand men in the second. The seasons were different. The events took place in different parts of the country (the first occurred on the northeast side of the Sea of Galilee; the second on the southeast shore). The amount of food before the miracles was different (five fish and two loaves in the first event; seven loaves and a "few small fish" in the second). The amount of "leftovers" differed (twelve baskets versus seven baskets). The term used for *basket* was different and referred to different sizes. And as mentioned, the nationalities of the crowd differed.

> Then Jesus said to them, "Most assuredly, I say to you, Moses did not give you the bread from heaven, but My Father gives you the true bread from heaven."
>
> John 6:32 NKJV

There was more symbolism. Jews considered bread a gift from God and the waste of it an affront to his goodness. Jews would recall the miraculous feeding God provided when Moses led the Jews through the wilderness of Sinai. But even more to the point, Jesus had been teaching he was the bread of life.

Myth Buster

Some see Jesus as just a Jewish prophet, but Jesus' view was far more expansive. While he went to the Jews first, he never shied away from Gentiles. Some of Jesus' most remarkable miracles were done for Gentile individuals. The early church struggled with this. Not long after the founding of the church, a debate arose about whether Gentiles must first become Jews to become Christians. It may sound silly today, but it was a tough issue two thousand years ago. The church realized there was no difference and reached out to everyone, Jews and Gentiles, just as Jesus did with these two miracles.

Final Thought

 We can look at the miracles of mass feeding as a two-act play. Taken together, we see Jesus' concern stretched across ethnic boundaries. He met the needs of Jews and Gentiles. When reading about the miracles we need to look at the details. That's where the heart of the lesson is.

Check Your Understanding

- **What is the primary purpose of a miracle?**

Trick question. There is no primary purpose. Every miracle achieves several things including providing an "object lesson" for the people of Jesus' day and for us.

- **Do the miracles of two thousand years ago have a bearing on us today?**

Absolutely. Jesus' miracles continue to inspire, authenticate his message, and teach us today. Every time we come to a biblical miracle, we come to an event that carries a lasting message.

- **Why was it important for Jesus to perform the same miracle for the Gentiles as for the Jews?**

The division between Gentiles and Jews in the first century was great. Jesus would die for the world, not one segment of the population. The Gentile mass feeding elevated the Gentiles in the eyes of the disciples and those who heard of it.

The World's Greatest Teacher

Jesus spent much of his time teaching, and his words have made their way into nearly every language. He taught in unusual but always unforgettable ways. Today people still learn from his lessons.

Contents

To the Jews who had believed him, Jesus said, "If you hold
to my teaching, you are really my disciples. Then you will
know the truth, and the truth will set you free."

John 8:31–32 NIV

Jesus' Parables

We are a story people. Whether it comes through a book, on a movie screen, beamed to our television, or appears in a magazine, a story sticks with us. Many of us have learned morals from the stories we have heard.

Jesus was a master storyteller. He often taught using tales loaded with meaning. We call those tales parables. *Parable* comes from a Greek word that means "to set beside" for comparison. The simplest definition of parable is a story told with two meanings. Jesus often used examples from everyday life to teach a spiritual truth.

Bible translator and writer J. B. Phillips wrote, "I sometimes wonder what hours of prayer and thought lie behind the apparently simple and spontaneous parables of the Gospels." On the surface, parables appear to be little more than simple stories, but Jesus used them to achieve several goals.

Some say a parable is an earthly story with a heavenly meaning. That's a good description. Jesus often used these little stories to get people to think. Drawing on actions and behavior common to the people of the day, Jesus would weave a tale that would have people talking for long after. When his disciples asked why he taught in parables, he gave an unexpected answer: so that some will understand and others will not (Mark 4:11-12). Seems odd. Wouldn't Jesus want everyone to understand his teaching? Of course, but not everyone was willing to listen.

Jesus spoke all these things to the crowd in parables; he did not say anything to them without using a parable.

Matthew 13:34 NIV

With many stories like these, he presented his message to them, fitting the stories to their experience and maturity. He was never without a story when he spoke. When he was alone with his disciples, he went over everything, sorting out the tangles, untying the knots.

Mark 4:33–34 MSG

Parables require thought. An effort must be made to understand them, and many of his listeners didn't want to go through the trouble of thinking. Understanding a parable often took time. Jesus' critics and enemies didn't come to hear but to criticize. Parables made such criticism more difficult.

In Jesus' day, a wheat farmer would gather grain by tossing it in the air repeatedly. The action would separate the wheat from its husk. The grain, being heavier, would fall to the ground; wind would carry away the light husks. After a time, only the edible part of the wheat remained. In many ways, a parable did the same thing. Those who cared to know listened closely and pondered the parable's meaning; those who didn't care stopped listening.

The Gospels record thirty parables. Jesus used examples drawn from agriculture, business, money, family, weddings, and more. Even people who have never crossed the threshold of a church know some of the parables. The parable of the prodigal son (Luke 15:11–32) is touching and heartwarming, reminding the listener that God is always ready to take back those who have turned away from him. The parable of the pearl of great price (Matthew 13:45–46) teaches that there are things more valuable than all our possessions. The parable of the sower (Matthew 13:3–8) describes how the kingdom of God spreads and how various people react to it.

In the Chapel of the Prodigal in Montreat, North Carolina, is a Ben Long fresco based on Jesus' parable. Like the parable, the painting is filled with subtle detail. The more one looks at the painting, the more one sees. The same is true for the parable that inspired the artwork. The more we think about a parable, the more truth seems to float to the top.

Events often triggered a parable teaching. Sometimes Jesus used parables as part of his preaching. Crowds would gather, Jesus would preach, then say, "The kingdom of heaven is like . . . ," and present a parable. Three times, Jesus gave parables to his disciples as part of their spiritual education. More than one-third of Jesus' parables were prompted by criticism from his opponents or by comments from the self-righteous, or they were answers to the verbal persecution of the religious leaders.

Teaching by parable wasn't new even in Jesus' day. It's an ancient practice that still has merit today. In the hands of Jesus, however, the parable reached a new height, prompting sermons, books, paintings, dramas, and music. In most U.S. states, there are good Samaritan laws. The name comes from one of Jesus' parables.

> I will open my mouth in a parable; I will utter dark sayings from of old, things that we have heard and known, that our ancestors have told us.
>
> Psalm 78:2–3 NRSV

Parables come across as simple things that Jesus pulled up at a moment's notice, but they are so much more. It takes effort to fully understand a parable and its details, and it is well worth the effort to do so.

Myth Buster

One of the myths about parables is that they are simple stories for simple people. The people of Jesus' day were not as simple as some would have us believe. They erected great buildings, lived in a pluralistic society, and many could speak several languages, including Aramaic, Hebrew, Greek, and Roman. There were banking systems, businesses, thriving agricultural operations, and much more. The people of Jesus' time were intelligent, witty, insightful thinkers. Jesus didn't tell parables to make truth simple; he told them to make his listeners work for their knowledge.

Final Thought

Parables are impossible to forget. They project a drama on our minds. In them, we see great truth in everyday occurrences. In many of them, we see people very much like ourselves, people who need encouragement, or correction, or forgiveness. Many parables are stories about common people told for common people.

Check Your Understanding

- **What is the basic meaning of the word *parable* and why is it important?**

Parable means to lay something beside another with the idea of comparing them. In this case, Jesus laid a common, repeatable story next to a heavenly truth so people could see and accept the truth being presented.

- **What does Jesus' use of parables tell us about his preaching/teaching style?**

Jesus used a variety of ways to communicate, from one-on-one conversations to sermons to parables. By combining various teaching techniques, Jesus made sure that his message would long be remembered.

- **Can you think of stories you heard as a child or in school that are still in your memory? Why do stories stay with us so long?**

It's part of our design. When we hear a story, we form a mental image and see the action in our minds. That extra effort makes a story difficult to forget.

The Rich Man and Lazarus—
A Different Kind of Story

Look at any list of parables, and you will find one called the rich man and Lazarus. We find the account in Luke 16:19–31. It is one of the best-known stories. But here's the catch: it might not be a parable at all. Technically, a parable is a small fictional story meant to carry a spiritual truth. This parable conveys spiritual truth all right, but it might be more of an account than a story.

✳

Why the confusion? It all stems from the use of a proper name. If this is a parable, then it is the only one in which Jesus used a personal name—Lazarus. Jesus refers to the other character only as "a rich man." Tradition tells us his name was Dives, but there is no biblical evidence of that.

The story is a contrast between Lazarus, a beggar, ill, forgotten, and ignored by the rich man. Lazarus led a miserable life in the shadow of others. He had no food, no medicine, and only dogs for company. (Dogs were not pets in Jesus' day and were unwanted animals.) Then death took both of them, and fortunes were reversed. The rich man woke up in a place of torment; Lazarus woke up in "Abraham's Bosom," a heavenly place. Gone were his sores, his disgrace, and his poverty. The rich man lost things too, everything he valued in life—comfort, peace, and respect. The lesson is almost too simple: life continues in the next life, and what we do now affects what happens then.

He will wipe every tear from their eyes, and there will be no more death or sorrow or crying or pain. All these things are gone forever.

Revelation 21:4 NLT

Surely goodness and mercy shall follow me all the days of my life, and I shall dwell in the house of the LORD my whole life long.

Psalm 23:6 NRSV

In some ways, the account doesn't read like a parable. There's no layered meaning. Jesus just tells the story as if he were an eyewitness. That has led some scholars to believe that the story Jesus tells is not fictive but is taken from a real event. There is no way to tell for certain, but the story is unique from all other parables.

Points to Remember

 Does it make a difference if the story is a fact and not a parable? No. Parables are tiny stories that teach unforgettable facts. Jesus' goal was to educate his listeners. This account certainly does just that.

Check Your Understanding

- **Assume the rich man and Lazarus were part of an actual event Jesus used to teach a heavenly truth. Does that change its value as a parable?**

Not at all. There's nothing that requires a parable to be made up. This story might be different from the parables, but that doesn't make it any less valuable.

- **How does the story's impact change if it is a true event?**

The truth in the story doesn't change, but the impact on the contemporary listener may be greater.

- **This story is one of role reversal. What does that teach us?**

The rich man lost everything for eternity; Lazarus gained everything for eternity. It teaches us that life does not end at death. Not only do we live, but we feel, think, and communicate.

Jesus' Sermon on the Mount

Sitting in a window seat of a commercial jet and flying at thirty-five thousand feet changes our perspective. Things that would normally seem large appear tiny. In a sense, flying gives us a "big picture" perspective of our world. Jesus' famous Sermon on the Mount does the same thing. Over his three-year ministry, Jesus would teach many things, but at the beginning, he delivered a grand summary of "kingdom life"—life lived with godly attitudes. Former White House speechwriter William Safire called the Sermon on the Mount the single most important discourse on Christian living. That is almost an understatement.

Matthew 5-7 contains Jesus' Sermon on the Mount, called such because it took place on one of the hills in Galilee. Most likely Jesus preached the sermon more than once and in different locations. It may well be the most famous speech ever given.

Early in Jesus' ministry, he gathered his new disciples around him for a lesson. They were not alone: a crowd had gathered. Jesus not only taught his disciples, but he also taught everyone present. The wide-ranging lesson touched on the key areas of life.

Jesus began with the Beatitudes. The word *beatitude* comes from *blessed*, a term Jesus used nine

Anyone who hears and obeys these teachings of mine is like a wise person who built a house on solid rock. Rain poured down, rivers flooded, and winds beat against that house. But it did not fall, because it was built on solid rock. Anyone who hears my teachings and doesn't obey them is like a foolish person who built a house on sand. The rain poured down, the rivers flooded, and the winds blew and beat against that house. Finally, it fell with a crash.

Matthew 7:24–27 CEV

times at the beginning of the message. *Blessed* means "happy," yet the phrases are ironic: blessed are those who are poor, mourning, meek, hungry, persecuted, and reviled. Doesn't seem like there is much to be happy about there, but Jesus balances each statement with promises of comfort, acceptance, filling, and more.

The Sermon on the Mount centers on relationship. First, it deals with how we relate to ourselves. Someone once called the Beatitudes the "beautiful attitudes." Each one is meant to provide encouragement. Then Jesus taught about our treatment of others. He covered murder, adultery, divorce, oaths, retribution, and the need to love our enemies. Next, he explained how to relate to God through giving and prayer. Last, Jesus provided guidelines for living in the world: storing up the right treasure, rejecting anxiety, refusing to be judgmental, knowing God hears prayers, and a warning about false teachers.

Take It to Heart

Billy Graham observed that the character we find in the Beatitudes is nothing less than Jesus' character put into words: "It is the description set side by side with an example." Jesus not only taught these principles, he lived them.

Check Your Understanding

- **How influential is the Sermon on the Mount?**

It is so influential that many people unknowingly use phrases from it in everyday life. Phrases like "salt of the earth," "let your light shine," "turn the other cheek," "love your enemies," and more come from that one sermon.

- **Is the Sermon on the Mount practical in our contemporary society?**

Absolutely. The sermon exemplifies a Christlike life. Jesus lived it in his day, and we can live it in ours. Our world would be greatly improved simply by practicing Jesus' teaching.

Jesus Teaches About God's Desire

John 3:16 may be the most famous verse in the Bible. The numbers alone carry the reader to a uniquely clear verse that has moved hearts and minds since the day it was uttered so many centuries ago. John 3:16–17 sums up Jesus and his mission. It also reveals the mind of God. Some are surprised to learn that the verses don't come from one of Jesus' sermons, but from a dialogue between him and a religious leader named Nicodemus. Nicodemus, a member of the Jewish ruling council, went to Jesus to learn more about him. Instead, he learned more about himself.

✳

Moved by the miracles he had seen, Nicodemus approached Jesus with praise: "Your miraculous signs are evidence that God is with you" (John 3:2 NLT). Jesus didn't respond to the compliment. Instead, he tossed out a provocative statement stating that no one could see the kingdom of God unless he was born again. Religious leaders of the day loved to debate, and Nicodemus was ready, or so he thought. He asked Jesus how a grown man could be born again. Nicodemus was thinking physically; Jesus was speaking spiritually. He pressed Nicodemus further and then made a startling statement:

"God so loved the world that he gave his only Son, so that everyone who believes in him may not perish but may have eternal life. Indeed, God did not send the Son into the world to condemn the world, but in order that the world might be saved through him" (John 3:16–17 NRSV).

The Lord is not slow in keeping his promise, as some understand slowness. He is patient with you, not wanting anyone to perish, but everyone to come to repentance.

2 Peter 3:9 NIV

This is good and pleases God our Savior, who wants everyone to be saved and to understand the truth.

1 Timothy 2:3–4 NLT

In those fifty-one words, Jesus told the world what God wants: salvation for all people. Jesus didn't mention a particular ethnic group; he mentioned the world. He described not a vengeful God, but a loving one—someone who was willing to send his Son as a sacrifice so the world wouldn't be condemned but saved. *Save* comes from a Greek word meaning "to rescue someone in trouble."

What God desired then is what he desires now: salvation, not condemnation. Jesus would provide the teaching, the example, and the sacrifice to make that possible. That's how much God loved Nicodemus. That's how much God loves the world today.

Final Thought

 That encounter changed Nicodemus. He appears in the Gospel of John only three times. The second time he appears, he defends Jesus to the council of which he was a member. We see him the last time when he and Joseph of Arimathea take responsibility for burying the body of Jesus.

Check Your Understanding

- **John 3:16–17 is the gospel in a nutshell. Why?**

The verses condense Jesus' message and purpose into just a few words, showing that Jesus came to be the sacrifice for the world and that God's desire is a restored relationship with people and takes no pleasure in condemnation.

- **Nicodemus belonged to a group of leaders who would later criticize and ultimately plan Jesus' death. What made him different?**

Salvation is a gift. Because a gift is offered doesn't mean it will be accepted. Nicodemus saw what Jesus offered and accepted it. Most of his fellow councilmen chose to reject Jesus.

Jesus Teaches About Our Need for Forgiveness

Forgiveness. The act carries great power, causes joy, releases burdens, opens doors, and heals wounds. Jesus taught forgiveness, practiced forgiveness, exemplified forgiveness. Nested in the Sermon on the Mount is the model prayer, a line of which reads, ". . . and forgive us our sins, as we have forgiven those who sin against us" (Matthew 6:12 NLT). Jesus then explained the line to his disciples, telling them we forgive because God has forgiven us. To be forgiven, Jesus taught, we first must be willing to forgive. That may be the most difficult thing Jesus tells us to do.

Forgiveness is a difficult task. Hurt feelings, anger, and depression can keep us from doing the very thing the Bible says will free us. Difficulty, however, does not negate the importance of forgiving those who have wronged us. Forgiveness is the only portion of the Lord's Prayer that comes with a condition.

Peter came to Jesus and asked how often he was required to forgive someone. Peter suggested seven times. How shocked he must have been when Jesus answered, "Seventy times seven" (Matthew 18:22 NLT). Jesus didn't mean a literal 490 times. He meant Peter was required to continue forgiving.

> Make allowance for each other's faults, and forgive anyone who offends you. Remember, the Lord forgave you, so you must forgive others.
>
> Colossians 3:13 NLT
>
> Be kind to one another, tenderhearted, forgiving one another, even as God in Christ forgave you.
>
> Ephesians 4:32 NKJV

For some, forgiving is just one step beyond impossible, yet not forgiving harms only the one who holds a grudge. Benjamin Franklin said, "Doing an injury puts you below your enemy; revenging one makes you but even with him; forgiving it sets you above him."

Jesus didn't teach that we must be doormats. In fact, he said if a brother sins against us, we are to rebuke him; if he repents, then we are to forgive him. Jesus withstood a constant barrage of escalating attacks. First came challenges, then lies, then conspiracy, then physical attacks. In the end, Jesus' enemies orchestrated a conspiracy that led to his crucifixion. At each turn, Jesus stood up to his detractors. He never backed away—but he also forgave all who asked. And he still does.

Final Thought

The pinnacle of forgiveness came in a handful of words uttered by Jesus as, in unimaginable agony, he prayed for God to forgive the ones who nailed him to the cross. As he hovered just above death, his greatest desire was to forgive his enemies. He is the ultimate example of forgiveness.

Check Your Understanding

- **Forgiveness has never been easy, but it is essential to a satisfied and happy life, and to pleasing God. What makes forgiveness so difficult?**

Humans are emotional beings, and an emotional injury often lasts longer than a physical one. Part of human nature is to return whatever pain we receive. Unfortunately, such actions solve nothing.

- **What is the greatest motivation to forgive?**

One is certainly the example of Jesus, who forgave as he hung on the cross. Another is the understanding that we too need to be forgiven by others and most of all by God.

Jesus Teaches About Our Responsibility to Others

A Southern California church undertook a ministry in Malawi, Africa, to help a village that lacked safe water. What little water they had was contaminated and had to be boiled and filtered for hours. The water carried disease. The average life span for members of the community was just thirty-seven years. The church made a decision to change the situation, committed to drilling six deep wells, and began to collect money for the process. They hoped to raise $40,000; they collected $180,000—more than four times as their original goal. The congregation knew they could make a difference and did so.

✵

The good Samaritan (Luke 10:25-37) is Jesus' most recognized parable. What many don't know is that the story came out of a confrontation. An expert in religious law asked a question: "Teacher, what shall I do to inherit eternal life?" (v. 25 NASB). Jesus answered with a question of his own: "What is written in the Law?" (v. 26 NASB). The man gave a twofold answer: love God, and love my neighbor as myself. Jesus agreed, but the man wasn't done. He asked, "And who is my neighbor?" (v. 29 NASB).

Jesus told of a man who, while traveling from Jerusalem to Jericho, was attacked by robbers, beaten, stripped, and left for dead. Jesus continued by saying a priest came upon the injured man but passed him by. Then a Levite came who

"Love the Lord your God with all your heart and with all your soul and with all your mind and with all your strength." The second is this: "Love your neighbor as yourself." There is no commandment greater than these.

Mark 12:30–31 NIV

If someone has enough money to live well and sees a brother or sister in need but shows no compassion—how can God's love be in that person?

1 John 3:17 NLT

did the same. Levites were men who helped the priests with temple duties. The assumption was that these were the most likely men to help, but neither did.

Then Jesus told how a Samaritan stopped and helped the fallen Jew, bandaged his wounds, transported him to an inn, and then paid the innkeeper for the room and the food the man would need during his recuperation. Jews hated Samaritans and considered them half-breeds with a corrupted religion, yet it was the Samaritan who took the time to help someone the religious leaders avoided.

Jesus then asked which of the three men proved to be a loving neighbor. There was only one answer: the Samaritan.

Take It to Heart

Jesus leveled the playing field. He avoided categorizing people by their heritage, judging them instead on their behavior. Many times, he taught or demonstrated that people have a responsibility to help others when they can, no matter how different they are. Our love for God is shown through our loving behavior.

Check Your Understanding

- **Why did Jesus use two religious leaders as examples of poor behavior?**

The man who asked the question was a religious lawyer, that is, someone who knew and taught the law of Moses to others, yet there were practical things he had failed to understand. Jesus put a "twist in the tale" by having a Samaritan as the hero.

- **What is the bottom line of Jesus' parable?**

That neighbors are more than those who agree with us, look like us, or behave like us. Everyone is our neighbor, and we have a responsibility to help when we can.

Jesus Teaches About Prayer

In the midst of the Sermon on the Mount, Jesus paused to teach about prayer. Prayer seems simple enough, yet Jesus felt the need to teach people how to do it. So there on the mount, Jesus recited words that have been uttered countless times through the centuries. Some call it the "Our Father"; others call it the Lord's Prayer; and still others refer to it as the model prayer. Whatever the title, the short example contains the desire of every believer. Less than seventy words long, it is as much a lesson in living as an example of communication with God.

Matthew 6:9–13 contains an outline for proper prayer. Often called the Lord's Prayer, many contemporary scholars refer to it as the model prayer because the text lays out an overview of prayer. The words we are so familiar with, "Our Father which art in heaven . . . ," come from the old King James Version. Many consider it some of the most beautiful prose ever written.

> Never stop praying. Be thankful in all circumstances, for this is God's will for you who belong to Christ Jesus.
>
> 1 Thessalonians 5:17–18 NLT
>
> Devote yourselves to prayer, keeping alert in it with thanksgiving.
>
> Colossians 4:2 NRSV

Jesus didn't recite the words to make literary history, however, but rather to teach people about prayer. A close look reveals a simple but powerful outline. First Jesus showed that when we pray we should address God, but notice how personal the address is: "Our Father" (Matthew 6:9 NKJV). It's personal. It's the way a child addresses a parent. Prayer is conversation between intimates. In the first eighteen verses of Matthew 6, Jesus uses the word *Father* ten times.

Then Jesus followed the address with the praise: "Hallowed be Your name" (v. 9 NKJV). The phrase shows a desire for God's name to be revered.

Sometimes we hear someone speak of God as the "old man upstairs" or by some other inaccurate phrase. Such comments, while usually made respectfully, dilute the proper view of the Holy God and Creator of the universe. Jesus taught that our desire is for God's name to be kept holy.

The next part of the prayer is a request that God's kingdom will spread across the earth and that his will be done everywhere. It reveals a yearning for God's will to be enacted on earth as it is in heaven.

Only after that do personal requests begin. "Give us this day our daily bread" (v. 11 NKJV) is prayer for the daily needs common to all of us. It isn't a prayer for wealth, but one for needs. Another need is forgiveness, and Jesus taught that we should ask for forgiveness when we pray and commit ourselves to forgive those who have sinned against us.

Another pair of personal requests follows the prayer for forgiveness: "Do not lead us into temptation" (v. 13 NKJV). People then as now were subject to temptations, and those concerned with their spiritual walk prayed for deliverance from temptation. The prayer includes the recognition of our weakness and need for God's strength to lead a holy life.

Prior to reciting the model prayer, Jesus warned the listeners against behavior that dilutes prayer. By Jesus' day, a practice of praying in public to be noticed had become common. Those who wanted praise for their piety would stand on the street corners to offer their prayers. Jesus taught that prayer was a private conversation between the person and God. Another prayer "crime" was meaningless repetition, uttering the same phrases repeatedly. This was a Gentile practice. Gentiles believed the gods would respond to their prayers if they just kept repeating them. Jesus' model of prayer was an honest sharing between two individuals—God and the one praying.

Another interesting facet of the model prayer is Jesus' use of plural pronouns: "our," "us," and "we." Although prayer takes place in private, except during worship services where the pastor utters prayer on behalf of the congregation, prayer involves others. Prayer isn't confined to our personal worship and requests but also includes the needs of others. Prayer for others is one of the noblest things a person can do.

There is nothing wrong with reciting the model prayer, but Jesus' intent was for us to see what quality prayer contains: praise for God; a heart for his kingdom; a way to make our needs known; a reminder that we need forgiveness and should forgive others; and that the strength to resist temptation comes through prayer.

> Confess your sins to each other and pray for each other so that you may be healed. The earnest prayer of a righteous person has great power and produces wonderful results.
>
> James 5:16 NLT

Every prayer begins with "Our Father" and ends with a request to be delivered from evil. Prayer has never been about informing God but about encountering him. "Prayer," Mother Teresa said, "enlarges the heart until it is capable of containing God's gift of himself."

Something to Ponder

James Hudson Taylor was a nineteenth-century missionary to China. He spent fifty-one years working in China, starting churches and 125 schools. About prayer he said, "I used to ask God to help me. Then I asked if I might help Him. I ended up by asking Him to do His work through me." Prayer changes the world by changing the one who prays. Prayer isn't uttering meaningless words; it is reaching into heaven and taking God's hand.

Prayer should never be one's last resort; it should always be one's first resource.

Final Thought

A prayer consisting only of requests is half a prayer. Jesus taught that every prayer should begin with praise for God and a seeking of his will. The goal of prayer isn't just to get something from God; it's to give something to God. Both actions are appropriate and encouraged in the Bible.

Check Your Understanding

- **Why do you suppose Jesus felt the need to teach people how to pray?**

In Jesus' day, prayer had fallen on hard times. For some, it had become a way to draw attention to themselves.

- **Has the need for prayer changed over the years since Jesus gave us the model prayer?**

Many things have changed, but God isn't one of them; nor has his desire to hear from his children changed. Prayer remains needed.

- **Why did Jesus teach that prayer should be done in private?**

Prayer is conversation with God. We do not pray to be heard by others, but by One: God.

Jesus Teaches About Our Relationship to Him

Students of comparative religions have noted that Christianity differs from other religions in the way its followers relate to God. While many religions show a god separated from his followers, the Bible indicates God's greatest desire is relationship with his creation. That relationship reached its pinnacle when Jesus came as a human, lived among people, and drew others to him. Relationship defines humanity. We have family relations, friends, coworkers, country affiliations, clubs, social groups, and many more means of connection. We crave relationship. It's part of being created in the image of God.

Jesus was a "people person." Jesus always made his way to where the people were so he could minister to them. In the process, Jesus forged relationships. A list of all those relationships would be long, but three stand out.

Disciples. A disciple is a person who follows the teaching of a master. When we see the word in the New Testament, we tend to think of the twelve men closest to Jesus, but he had many other disciples. Luke 10:1 mentions seventy men whom Jesus sent out on a mission. After Jesus' death and resurrection, Peter stood and addressed a group of 120 disciples (Acts 1:15). The word applies to any follower of Jesus. We are learners, students of all that Jesus did and said.

The greatest way to show love for friends is to die for them. And you are my friends, if you obey me. Servants don't know what their master is doing, and so I don't speak to you as my servants. I speak to you as my friends, and I have told you everything that my Father has told me.

John 15:13–15 CEV

Stretching out His hand toward His disciples, He said, "Behold My mother and My brothers! For whoever does the will of My Father who is in heaven, he is My brother and sister and mother."

Matthew 12:49–50 NASB

Friends. Jesus is God in the flesh, so it seems odd to refer to him as our friend, yet he was the one who made that distinction. *Friend* is the term we use to describe people we like and who like us. In the Upper Room Discourse (John 13–17), a sermon delivered to the disciples shortly before he was arrested, Jesus said, "I have called you friends" (15:15 NASB). Such a statement is a high compliment.

Brothers. If any relationship is more important than friendship, it's family. Matthew 12:49 shows Jesus motioning to those gathered around him and calling them "my mother and my brothers" (NIV). Jesus brought us into the family. It's the reason Christians refer to one another as brother and sister.

Take It to Heart

Psychologists have long known that people need relationships. Jesus brought the highest relationship available to us: a relationship with God. Not a master-slave association, but one that treats us as beloved students, welcome friends, close family. Jesus came to draw us in, not to keep us out.

Check Your Understanding

- **Why are these relationships significant? Does it matter?**

It matters a great deal. Many people have the misguided impression that Christianity teaches that people are unimportant sinners. Jesus taught that we are loved family.

- **How does this knowledge change our view of Jesus?**

One change is the way we see Jesus. When viewed properly, we see Jesus not as judgmental, but as a loving Savior who desires that each of us be in a relationship with him.

Jesus Teaches About His Death and Resurrection

A father and his adult son faced a difficult time. Doctors told the father he had an incurable disease and suggested he get his affairs in order. His son, a well-known writer, tried to comfort him. He said, "Dad, we're all dying. You just know how soon." The son wasn't being cruel; he simply wanted his father to understand that death comes to everyone. Still, knowing that death is around the corner is far more startling than knowing that it awaits us somewhere in the murky future. Jesus knew exactly when and where he would die—and he went there anyway.

Matthew records four occurrences when Jesus told his disciples about the arrest, abuse, and death that awaited him (12:40; 16:21; 17:22–23). On one of his trips to Jerusalem, Jesus took the twelve disciples aside and said, "We are going up to Jerusalem, and the Son of Man will be handed over to the chief priests and scribes, and they will condemn him to death; then they will hand him over to the Gentiles to be mocked and flogged and crucified; and on the third day he will be raised" (Matthew 20:18-19 NRSV).

Jesus taught not only that he would die in Jerusalem but how. First, he identified the chief priests and scribes as the conspirators who would orchestrate his execution. Chief priests were a prestigious group of temple priests drawn from the upper

> [God's] prearranged plan was carried out when Jesus was betrayed. With the help of lawless Gentiles, you nailed him to a cross and killed him. But God released him from the horrors of death and raised him back to life, for death could not keep him in its grip.
>
> Acts 2:23–24 NLT
>
> [Jesus] said to His disciples, "You know that after two days is the Passover, and the Son of Man will be delivered up to be crucified."
>
> Matthew 26:1–2 NKJV

strata of Jerusalem's society. Jesus also mentioned the scribes, men who preserved and taught biblical Jewish law. Jesus told the disciples before-hand that these men would condemn him to death.

Since Rome ruled the land, the Jewish leaders did not have the author-ity to execute anyone; Jesus, therefore, would be handed over to the "Gentiles." The Romans would examine Jesus, mock him, and flog him. Finally, they would nail him to a cross. But that wouldn't be the end of the story—he would be resurrected. It's one thing to say, "People are going to kill me," and quite another to say, "But I'll come back to life after being dead for three days."

Points to Remember

It's important to remember that Jesus not only taught about his impending death, but he did so in detail, listing the groups who would conspire against him, the Roman involvement, and the means of execution. He also taught that the impossible—his resurrection—would happen and what day it would happen on.

Check Your Understanding

- **Why would Jesus repeatedly teach about his death and resurrection?**

Jesus taught about his death and resurrection first to prepare his disci-ples for the horrible events to come; second to show his death and resurrection were part of God's plan and not a thwarting of it; and last, to show his willingness to sacrifice himself for humankind.

- **Did knowing his death was coming make it easier on Jesus?**

Not in the least. The Gospels show the ever-increasing weight on Jesus' shoulders and the agony such knowledge brought him. Jesus' suffer-ing began long before his arrest and crucifixion.

Jesus Teaches About His Second Coming

The book arrived in the mail to the surprise of the church leader. He had ordered no books, and yet there it was, a package that clearly held a book. Back in his office, the minister opened the parcel and found a book written by a former NASA engineer. After years of study and using higher math, the engineer had finally nailed down the day when Jesus would return. That was in the mid-1980s. The engineer, like countless people before him, believed the date of Jesus' return could be predicted. So far, no one has been right.

✳

Jesus promised to return and taught his disciples about the matter. One thing he never did, however, was reveal a date. In fact, he taught that no one could know the date. He said to his disciples, "No one knows about that day or hour, not even the angels in heaven, nor the Son, but only the Father" (Matthew 24:36 NIV). He added, "So you also must be ready, because the Son of Man will come at an hour when you do not expect him" (v. 44 NIV). These are two statements from Jesus himself telling us that no one knows the date and that his return could happen any minute.

Not knowing a date does not dismiss the idea of Jesus' return. The subject has been the topic of countless books. It's an important topic but one with limited conclu-

Our citizenship is in heaven, and it is from there that we are expecting a Savior, the Lord Jesus Christ. He will transform the body of our humiliation that it may be conformed to the body of his glory, by the power that also enables him to make all things subject to himself.

Philippians 3:20–21 NRSV

They speak of how you are looking forward to the coming of God's Son from heaven—Jesus, whom God raised from the dead. He is the one who has rescued us from the terrors of the coming judgment.

1 Thessalonians 1:10 NLT

sions. Jesus taught as fact that he would return to heaven but someday return. That return would be physical, sudden, and seen by the world. Three of the Gospels record Jesus' words about his return: Matthew 24-25; Mark 13:1-37; Luke 21:5-36. These rather lengthy discourses, coupled with Old Testament prophecies, references in the letters of the New Testament, and John's book of Revelation, make an entire course of study. Some Bible colleges offer full-semester classes on the matter. Still, certain key elements can be plucked from Jesus' lesson to his disciples.

Jesus promised to return. "If I go and prepare a place for you, I will come again and receive you to Myself, that where I am, there you may be also" (John 14:3 NASB). He made this promise after mentioning his need to leave (the ascension). The apostles preached Jesus' return as part of their gospel message. Jesus said he'd return, and they believed him.

He will come in the clouds. As Jesus ascended into the clouds, so he will return in the clouds. "The sign that the Son of Man is coming will appear in the heavens, and there will be deep mourning among all the peoples of the earth. And they will see the Son of Man coming on the clouds of heaven with power and great glory" (Matthew 24:30 NLT). Everyone will see his return.

He will not return alone. Angels will accompany him. "When the Son of Man comes in his glory, and all the angels with him, then he will sit on the throne of his glory" (Matthew 25:31 NRSV). He will also return with his "saints," those believers who have already died. "May he, as a result, make your hearts strong, blameless, and holy as you stand before God our Father when our Lord Jesus comes again with all his holy people. Amen" (1 Thessalonians 3:13 NLT).

He will return unexpectedly. Matthew, Mark, and Luke each record Jesus promising his return would be without warning. The world will be going about its daily business just as it has for centuries. Then Jesus will return and everything will change.

The study of end times (eschatology) is demanding and complicated. There are scores (some count hundreds) of biblical comments and

> With a loud command and with the shout of the chief angel and a blast of God's trumpet, the Lord will return from heaven. Then those who had faith in Christ before they died will be raised to life. Next, all of us who are still alive will be taken up into the clouds together with them to meet the Lord in the sky. From that time on we will all be with the Lord forever. Encourage each other with these words.
>
> 1 Thessalonians 4:16–18 CEV

prophecies concerning Jesus' second coming, but they all can be reduced to a simple line: followers of Jesus need to be ready at all times. Jesus could return today or several centuries from now. Jesus called his disciples to be alert, anticipating the day when he would return. They lived their lives as if every new day would be that day. Such expectations did not keep them from doing the work that needed doing. They also knew that Jesus might not come back as soon as they would like, and they wanted to be found being busy.

Early followers of Jesus who believed in and longed for Jesus' return used to greet and say good-bye with the Aramaic word *maranatha*. It means "Our Lord, come." It was a prayer for Jesus' speedy return.

Myth Buster

A young woman in high school refused to study for tests. It was her senior year, and the tests were important. When asked why she wouldn't study she said, "Because Jesus is coming soon, and I won't need all of this." That was in 1971. The early Christians never used the reality of the second coming as an excuse not to be busy about the matters of life and work. And since, by Jesus' testimony, it is impossible to know when his return will be, assuming it's just around the corner shows little respect for the biblical teaching.

Final Thought

Jesus foretold his betrayal, and he was betrayed. Jesus foretold his arrest and trial, and he was arrested and tried. Jesus said he would be killed, and he was hanged on a cross. He said he would rise from the dead, and he did. Jesus said he would return—there's no reason to doubt him.

Check Your Understanding

- **Jesus often spoke of future events, especially when they concerned what would happen in his ministry. He also predicted the destruction of the temple, which occurred forty years after his death. How does that relate to his second coming?**

We trust those who have been truthful with us in the past. Everything Jesus said would happen did, with the exception of the second coming, which remains a future event. Since he proved himself so accurate on every other matter, we can trust him on this.

- **Why do you suppose Jesus hasn't returned yet?**

We can't say for certain, but Jesus' goal was and is the redemption of people. Every day he delays his return is another day for people to connect to him. Still, every day brings us closer to the most important event in history.

- **Is the return of Jesus a positive or negative event in your life?**

Hopefully, it's a positive one. The early Christians longed for the day when they would see Jesus face-to-face.

Private Sermons to the Disciples

Crowds followed Jesus, sometimes to such an extent that walking was difficult. Many came because of needs; others came to see miracles; still others came to hear all that Jesus had to say. The Gospels tell us that he taught with unusual authority (Luke 4:32). Some teaching, however, Jesus reserved for his close circle of twelve disciples. When Jesus began teaching in parables, he revealed special insights to just his disciples. After Jesus' resurrection and ascension, his disciples would become apostles—Jesus' representatives on earth. The difficult, life-threatening work they would do required special instruction.

Jesus often withdrew with his disciples to tutor them. The Gospel of John provides the longest record of one of these meetings. It extends over five chapters (13–17). In the upper room, a rented hall on the second floor of a large home, Jesus gave last-minute instructions. His betrayal, arrest, torture, and death were only hours away.

With his men gathered around a large table, Jesus took bread and wine and symbolically portrayed his coming death. Christians reenact Jesus' actions by celebrating the Lord's Supper, sometimes called the Eucharist or Holy Communion. Jesus took bread, broke it, and said it was his broken body. The wine, he said, was the blood he was about to shed.

Jesus, now well on the way up to Jerusalem, took the Twelve off to the side of the road and said, "Listen to me carefully. . . ."

Matthew 20:17–18 MSG

When Jesus had finished giving these instructions to his twelve disciples, he went out to teach and preach in towns throughout the region.

Matthew 11:1 NLT

Jesus washed the feet of his disciples, a task not even a Jewish slave could be commanded to do. Yet Jesus took a towel and a bowl of water, knelt before his followers, and washed their feet. He was teaching that humility was part of the Christian life and ministry.

Jesus followed those actions with a condensed lecture that predicted his death and resurrection, taught them to love one another, comforted the disciples, commanded unity, lectured about the coming Holy Spirit, told the disciples that he was the vine and they were the branches, warned them about the dangers ahead, spoke of his betrayal, then prayed for them and the world.

All of this he did with the knowledge that in a few hours he would be hanging on a cross.

Final Thought

 Jesus never overlooked the individual. Jesus' private meetings with the disciples were meant to encourage, inspire, and motivate. Jesus' teachings are recorded in the Bible for the same reason. When we prayerfully read about the life and teaching of Jesus, we are having a private meeting with him.

Check Your Understanding

■ **What would motivate Jesus to give private instruction to his disciples?**

The crowds were not ready for all that Jesus had to teach. Even the disciples had trouble understanding some of the things Jesus taught. Because of this teaching, however, the twelve disciples would be equipped to lead the church when the time came.

■ **These private lessons have been recorded in the Bible. Why?**

Contemporary followers of Jesus are disciples too, needing the same instruction the first disciples received.

Jesus' Final Message

On the Fourth of July, 1939, 61,808 people gathered at Yankee Stadium to say good-bye to a legend. Lou Gehrig—the man who set a record for the most consecutive baseball games played, a record that would last for sixty years—was leaving baseball. Stricken with ALS, "Lou Gehrig's disease," he could no longer play. He gave a short speech calling himself the "luckiest man on the face of the earth." When he walked from the field, sixty thousand people chanted, "We love you." It was an emotional moment for everyone. Gehrig's goal? To encourage the people who came to encourage him.

Jesus and the disciples had to say good-bye, and it was no easier. They had spent three years with him, seen him betrayed, brutalized, and killed. Three days later, they saw the empty grave and the resurrected Jesus. Now it was time for Jesus to pass the baton to the disciples. Jesus did so with a few short comments.

Matthew 28:18–20 is often called the Great Commission because Jesus gave marching orders to his disciples. His comments were few, approximately sixty words in English. First, Jesus spoke of himself, saying that all authority in heaven and earth had been given to him, making the point that the suffering portion of his ministry was over.

He told the disciples what he expected of them in the years ahead.

> You will receive power when the Holy Spirit has come upon you; and you will be my witnesses in Jerusalem, in all Judea and Samaria, and to the ends of the earth.
>
> Acts 1:8 NRSV

> He opened their understanding, that they might comprehend the Scriptures. Then He said to them, "Thus it is written, and thus it was necessary for the Christ to suffer and to rise from the dead the third day, and that repentance and remission of sins should be preached in His name to all nations, beginning at Jerusalem. And you are witnesses of these things."
>
> Luke 24:45–48 NKJV

They were to go and make disciples of all nations. For men who had never traveled from their country, it must have seemed an overwhelming task. They were to baptize new believers in the name of the Father, the Son, and the Holy Spirit.

Throughout Jesus' earthly ministry, the disciples had been students, and now they would be teachers. What were they supposed to teach? Everything Jesus had taught them. He commanded his disciples to make disciples.

Jesus' final words were encouraging: "I am with you always, even to the end of the age" (Matthew 28:20 NASB). Jesus might have been leaving their sight, but he would always be with them in spiritual ways. Not even time would change that.

Final Thought

 Jesus' final message told the disciples to begin the global work of building the church. Jesus' purpose was to call people back to a fellowship with God and to provide a sacrifice for sin. Two thousand years later, the message has gone into every country in the world.

Check Your Understanding

- **What do you suppose it was like for the disciples to hear Jesus' final earthly message?**

Certainly there was sadness, but Jesus had told them several times the day was coming. They must have felt some apprehension at the work they were about to begin.

- **Do you think the disciples felt abandoned?**

There's no evidence of it. Within a few months, the church in Jerusalem would be established with more than three thousand people responding to Peter's message. Jesus was gone from sight but not gone from their lives.

Friends and Enemies

Jesus polarized those who met him. Some loved him and became ardent followers; others hated him and became bitter enemies. Everyone had an opinion.

Contents

If the world hates you, you know that it
has hated Me before it hated you.

John 15:18 NASB

Mary Magdalene and Other Women Who Followed Jesus

When people picture Jesus, they often envision him walking the dirt roads of the Holy Land surrounded by his twelve disciples. The image isn't wrong, but neither is it complete. Jesus had women followers. Some of his support came from women of means. One such woman is famous, but the others remain shrouded in the shadows of history. These women played an important part in Jesus' work. While it might be going too far to call them disciples in the sense we use the word with Peter, James, John, and the others, they were certainly students and devoted followers.

Walter Winchell said, "A real friend is one who walks in when the rest of the world walks out." It's interesting to note that while Jesus hung on the cross, only one of his disciples, John, stood nearby. All others were women. Some of the women who followed Jesus showed great courage; they had the ability to be friends who walk in when everyone else walks out.

Mary Magdalene. Mary Magdalene may be one of the most famous women in the Bible and perhaps the world. She has been the subject of speculation and wonder. All we know of her comes from biblical accounts. Her name is first in every list of women associated with Jesus, and she may have been their leader,

There is neither Jew nor Greek, slave nor free, male nor female, for you are all one in Christ Jesus. If you belong to Christ, then you are Abraham's seed, and heirs according to the promise.

Galatians 3:28–29 NIV

There stood by the cross of Jesus His mother, and His mother's sister, Mary the wife of Clopas, and Mary Magdalene.

John 19:25 NKJV

much as Peter seemed to be the chief disciple. Her "last name" is a variation of the phrase "of Magdala." Magdala was a town near the Sea of

Galilee. She was afflicted with "seven demons" according to Luke 8:2. She followed Jesus from the earliest days of his ministry to the cross and after the resurrection. Like some of the other women, she supported the ministry financially (Luke 8:3). Her name appears in the Gospels eleven times and always in some key way. Her courage and commitment are remarkable.

Mary the mother of James. The name "Mary" appears fifty-five times in the Bible. There appear to be six people in the Gospels named Mary. The name was extremely popular in Jesus' day. We know very little of Mary the mother of James other than that she was at the cross (Mark 15:40) and at the empty tomb of Jesus (Mark 15:47). She, like the others, had come to add spices to Jesus' body.

Salome. Salome, whose name means "peace," shouldn't be confused with the Salome who danced before Herod and then as a reward called for the head of John the Baptist. This Salome stood near the cross and went to the tomb that first Easter morning.

Joanna the wife of Chuza. Joanna lived in a unique social setting. Her husband was a steward to Herod Antipas, one of the Jewish political leaders. A steward was a ranking servant. There is no way to determine if he was a household steward or a political steward to Herod. Herod Antipas was the son of Herod the Great, who called for the death of the infants in Bethlehem in an effort to have the baby Jesus killed (Matthew 2:16). During Jesus' trials, Pilate sent Jesus to Antipas, who sat in judgment of him. It's ironic and revealing that the wife of one of Herod Antipas's stewards was a follower of Jesus.

Mary the wife of Clopas. Mary the wife of Clopas (John 19:25), like many women who followed Jesus, is a mystery other than that she was at the foot of the cross as Jesus hung exposed and dying.

Susanna. Susanna was one of the women who ministered to Jesus and the others financially, giving of her means to support Jesus' work.

Other women. Luke 24:10 mentions "other women" (NKJV). We don't know their names or their activities, but we do know they provided support and were believers. Some scholars call these women the "female disciples," and the description seems to fit. Some may have traveled with Jesus the full three years of his ministry; others may have joined him whenever he was near their cities. They provided valuable service, showed courage, gave of their finances and of themselves, and may have had more to do with the spread of the gospel than we know. In an era where women had limited influence in religious, political, or business matters, these women stepped out of the mold to make a difference, and Jesus freed them to do so.

> They were Mary Magdalene and Joanna and Mary the mother of James; also the other women with them were telling these things to the apostles.
>
> Luke 24:10 NASB

Myth Buster

One of the myths that haunt Christianity is that it suppresses women and glorifies men. The truth is, early Christianity liberated women in many ways. The apostle Paul wrote there was neither "male nor female; for you are all one in Christ Jesus" (Galatians 3:28 NIV). It is true that society has taken longer to reach that understanding and that there are times in history where even the church lost sight of the all-inclusiveness of Christianity. Still, Jesus elevated women and valued them. The women mentioned above are examples of the openness of Jesus to both genders.

Final Thought

Aside from Mary Magdalene, very few of the women mentioned are known except to ardent Bible students, yet their activities earn them a place in a book that has lasted nearly two thousand years, and their names remind us that one doesn't have to be famous to make a difference.

Check Your Understanding

- **There is no doubt that women in Jesus' day did not enjoy the same freedom as men. Why did Jesus allow such a high level of participation from women when others would certainly notice it?**

Jesus did not come to conform to the world but to conform the world to him. He brought many changes that earned him many enemies. Still he did what was right. The criticisms of others never changed his course.

- **How influential were these women in the spread of Christianity?**

We don't know. We never hear of them again, but that doesn't mean they had no influence. The New Testament letters of Paul mention women who had churches in their homes or did other work. See Romans 16:1 and Colossians 4:15.

- **Were women always on the sidelines?**

Surprising for the day, no. Acts 18 mentions the apostle Paul and the support he received from Priscilla and Aquila, including their participation on a missionary journey. What makes this interesting is that, against custom, Priscilla's name is mentioned first in every reference. That honor usually went to the man.

Supporters and Followers—
Mary, Martha, and Lazarus

Winston Churchill forged a friendship with FDR. It was a friendship forged in the fires of World War II. He said about the U.S. president, "Meeting Franklin Roosevelt was like opening your first bottle of champagne; knowing him was like drinking it." Reading about Jesus' relationship with Mary, Martha, and Lazarus, we get the idea that they enjoyed one another's company. These friends were family members who lived in the small town of Bethany just a few miles from Jerusalem. Jesus would stay with the family whenever he traveled to Jerusalem.

While it isn't stated, Martha appears to be the oldest of the three. Luke 10:38-42 says Martha welcomed Jesus into *her* home. "Her home" indicates that she was the owner and that her sister Mary and brother Lazarus shared the home with her. The passage shows Martha to be a busy person. While Jesus taught, Martha stayed busy preparing food for the mob of people in her living room. Hospitality was important in her day, and she wanted everything to be right.

A friend is always a friend, and relatives are born to share our troubles.

Proverbs 17:17 CEV

Mary was the polar opposite of Martha. While Martha worked, Mary sat at Jesus' feet, listening to every word. Apparently, she couldn't pull herself away. When Martha complained, Jesus took Mary's side, saying she had made the better choice.

Jesus and the ones he makes holy have the same Father. That is why Jesus is not ashamed to call them his brothers and sisters.

Hebrews 2:11 NLT

We know Lazarus as the man who died, was entombed, and days later was brought back to life. In John 11:5, we learn that Jesus "loved" Mary, Martha, and Lazarus. The sisters had sent for Jesus, but he arrived too late. Lazarus had already been in the tomb for four days. The shortest verse in the Bible is John 11:35: "Jesus wept" (NASB). He wept at his friend's tomb even though he would bring Lazarus back to life. Why? He was moved by the sorrow of the sisters.

Jesus shared happiness and grief with these three. Jesus didn't call any of them to be part of his disciple circle, but they were disciples nonetheless, and perhaps even more important, friends.

Final Thought

 Many see Jesus as just an itinerant preacher who traveled from place to place too busy to form relationships. The Gospels show a different Jesus, one who sought out and enjoyed the company of others but who never lost sight of his mission. Jesus as friend is a comforting image.

Check Your Understanding

- **What does it mean that Jesus loved Mary, Martha, and Lazarus, all very different people?**

Jesus' love is all-encompassing. He loved all who came to him, and people who differed in many ways were drawn to him.

- **Did Jesus want Martha to be more like Mary?**

Jesus wanted Martha to see that some things are more important than others. In this case, it was more important that she spend time with Jesus as Mary did, but he wasn't asking her to change her personality.

Joseph of Arimathea and the Body of Jesus

Multimillionaire John D. Rockefeller, the wealthiest man of his day, said, "I have made many millions, but they have brought me no happiness. I would barter them all for the days I sat on an office stool in Cleveland and counted myself rich on three dollars a week." Many wealthy people have learned that riches can bring many things, but not happiness or a satisfied soul. Joseph of Arimathea found his purpose in a single, selfless act. That act probably cost him a great deal more than money.

Sometimes a single event can make a difference in our lives, but usually it is a chain of events that alters our behavior. Joseph of Arimathea is a famous man, but he is not remembered for his social work, his wealth, or his popularity. His great claim to fame was stepping out of the shadows to do something few would consider.

Very little is known about Joseph. We don't know his age, although it is reasonable to assume that he was middle-aged or older. We don't know whether he had a family or what he did for a living. We know he came from Arimathea, but the town's location is uncertain. Still, we do have some interesting information about him.

He is mentioned once in each of the four Gospels (Matthew 27:57; Mark 15:43; Luke 23:51; John 19:38). Nicodemus, who helped him, is mentioned only in John. Although each

> If anyone is ashamed of me and my words, the Son of Man will be ashamed of him when he comes in his glory and in the glory of the Father and of the holy angels.
>
> Luke 9:26 NIV

> I tell you, everyone who acknowledges me before others, the Son of Man also will acknowledge before the angels of God; but whoever denies me before others will be denied before the angels of God.
>
> Luke 12:8–9 NRSV

Gospel tells his story, he doesn't appear until after the death of Jesus. It's clear that he had had some kind of contact with Jesus and perhaps heard him teach on a number of occasions. Matthew called him a disciple, but he was a secret disciple.

Why a secret disciple? John wrote, "Joseph of Arimathea, being a disciple of Jesus, but a secret one for fear of the Jews, asked Pilate that he might take away the body of Jesus; and Pilate granted permission" (John 19:38 NASB). Fear of the Jews? The reference to Jews here and elsewhere in the New Testament refers to *Jewish*, not to every Jew. After all, Joseph was a Jew, as were Jesus and all the disciples.

What did he have to fear? Mark gives us the insight: "Joseph of Arimathea came, a prominent member of the Council, who himself was waiting for the kingdom of God; and he gathered up courage and went in before Pilate, and asked for the body of Jesus" (Mark 15:43 NASB). "Council" refers to a group of religious leaders who served as a Jewish supreme court in religious matters. Most of the council members were opposed to Jesus and orchestrated his death. To align himself with Jesus put him at odds with a group willing to murder an innocent man.

Luke called him "a good and upright man" (Luke 23:50 NIV), high praise in a legalistic society. Luke also mentioned Joseph "was waiting for the kingdom of God" (Luke 23:51 NASB). Mark noted the same thing. Waiting for the kingdom of God means Joseph was looking for the Messiah. He had come to believe Jesus was the Messiah he was waiting for.

Joseph had another distinction: he was wealthy. The Bible gives no explanation about how he came into his wealth. Whatever the source, he was known for his wealth, and it appears that wealth had not satisfied his soul. Rockefeller learned money could bring many things, but it wasn't a guarantee of happiness. Joseph learned the same thing. He had a comfortable life, but he was spiritually unhappy. He found spiritual peace in Jesus, a man who had no money and was supported by those around him.

Joseph might have been happy to stay in the shadows had Jesus not been killed when he had. Ancient Jews had strict rules about burial. To make matters worse, the sun was setting, which was the beginning of the Sabbath. Jesus had to be buried quickly, and Joseph could make it happen. Joseph gathered up his courage and stepped out of the shadows. First, he went to Pilate and asked for the body of Jesus. That simple act would forever link Joseph to Jesus in the eyes of Pilate and the ruling Jews. Since time was short, he and Nicodemus took control of the situation, retrieved Jesus' body, prepared it for burial, then placed it in Joseph's own family tomb—a new, never-used tomb.

> I am not ashamed, for I know whom I have believed and am persuaded that He is able to keep what I have committed to Him until that Day.
>
> 2 Timothy 1:12 NKJV

Digging Deeper

What happened to Joseph? We're not told. He's never mentioned again. Perhaps he joined the early church in Jerusalem; perhaps he went back to Arimathea. There is little doubt that he left the council. Persecution would soon come to the church, first from the religious leaders, then from Rome. He certainly witnessed the persecution and perhaps experienced it firsthand. Matthew 27:60 says Joseph rolled a large stone in front of the tomb and simply "went away" (NASB). Joseph's garden tomb became the most famous place on earth—the place where Jesus would appear resurrected and alive once again.

Final Thought

There are no secret followers. Events compelled Joseph out of his "spiritual hiding place" to stand among other believers. Jesus needed a burial place, and Joseph could provide one, but that required a public identification with Jesus—something he was willing to do.

Check Your Understanding

- **Do you suppose there were many secret disciples in Jesus' day?**

Considering the controversy that surrounded Jesus and the dangers to the early Christians, there must certainly have been many secret disciples. Still, the majority of believers followed Jesus without shame. The same is true today.

- **Why would someone be a secret disciple today?**

Reasons for being a secret disciple today include fear of social loss, confrontation by those who oppose Christianity, and, in some cases, family pressures.

- **Is it all right to be a secret disciple?**

Everyone Jesus called, he called publicly. We have no record of Jesus' scolding someone for choosing the shadows. Being a Christian involves going to church and being with other believers. It's impossible to be active in the Christian faith and keep it secret.

Out of the Shadows—
Nicodemus and Jesus' Burial

A pastor asked his congregation if they knew what a mugwump was. Getting no response he said, "A mugwump is a bird that sits on a fence with its mug on one side and its wump on the other." When someone calls another a "fence-sitter," he isn't paying a compliment. The term refers to someone who refuses to commit to a decision. We met one such person earlier, a religious leader named Nicodemus. A man of influence, he is mentioned only in the Gospel of John and then only three times (John 3:1–2; 7:50–52; 19:39).

✳

He first went to Jesus at night with a question, and then later made a halfhearted effort to ward off heated accusations made by his fellow religious leaders. It appears that Nicodemus had become a "secret" follower, someone who believed in Jesus but refused to publicly commit to him. It's difficult to blame him. Every day the anger of Jesus' enemies grew. They not only despised him, but they also despised everyone associated with him. Pressed with the desire to do the right thing but still avoid conflict, Nicodemus sat firmly on the fence. Until the crucifixion.

Jesus' death brought him out of the shadows. Along with Joseph of Arimathea, Nicodemus assumed responsibility for Jesus' body. Since Jesus was crucified, he would be considered a criminal. If the family

There was a man of the Pharisee sect, Nicodemus, a prominent leader among the Jews.

John 3:1 MSG

Nicodemus (he who came to Jesus by night, being one of them) said to them, "Does our law judge a man before it hears him and knows what he is doing?" They answered and said to him, "Are you also from Galilee? Search and look, for no prophet has arisen out of Galilee."

John 7:50–52 NKJV

of the crucified did not or could not assume responsibility for the body, then soldiers would take it outside the walls of Jerusalem to the trash dump and leave it to decay. Taking charge of the body required Nicodemus to come out of the shadows. It was one thing to approach Jesus at night, another thing to defend him behind the closed doors of the Jewish court, but taking responsibility for Jesus' body put him in the spotlight.

Nicodemus brought nearly a hundred pounds of oils and spices. Together the men washed, wrapped, and placed the body in the tomb; covered it with the spices—and then they rolled a large stone in front of the tomb's opening to seal it.

We never hear of Nicodemus again.

Final Thought

 By definition, a catalyst is something that brings about a change. In chemistry, it is a chemical that accelerates a reaction. Jesus was a catalyst in every human mind and soul. Meeting him brought about a change that eventually came out in public.

Check Your Understanding

- **Why didn't Nicodemus remain in the shadows after Jesus' crucifixion?**

Nicodemus was an honorable man and couldn't remain hidden after seeing what Jesus endured for the world. Sometimes circumstances call us to be braver than we are.

- **Nicodemus was a religious leader, part of the group that conspired against Jesus. What does this prove?**

It proves that not every religious leader opposed Jesus and that many saw in him the hope they had longed for and recognized him as the Messiah.

Those Who Hated Him Most—The Pharisees

Republicans, Democrats, Independents, Peace and Freedom . . . The names are familiar. Most adults belong to one political party or another. Those who follow politics know these groups often have different agendas and spend a lot of time arguing and positioning their party for greater success. Partisanship is nothing new. The first century saw its share of groups who felt they knew what was best for everyone else. One such group, and perhaps the most powerful in Jesus' day, were the Pharisees.

The Pharisees were a powerful and influential group. They began a couple of centuries before Jesus and seemed to pass in the first century AD. No one is certain what the name *Pharisee* means or how it originated. Some believe it means "separated ones," that is, individuals who have separated themselves from anything or anyone considered unholy. In a sense, when compared with other groups, they were the religious conservatives. They appear in the New Testament frequently with the name of their group mentioned ninety-eight times. They valued the books of Moses and had their own set of standards and practices. The Pharisees in Jesus' time believed in religious purity—a religious purity they defined. Those who didn't measure up were targets of ridicule.

I warn you—unless your righteousness is better than the righteousness of the teachers of religious law and the Pharisees, you will never enter the Kingdom of Heaven!

Matthew 5:20 NLT

All the tax collectors and the sinners drew near to Him to hear Him. And the Pharisees and scribes complained, saying, "This Man receives sinners and eats with them."

Luke 15:1–2 NKJV

They were legalists. A pastor described a legalist as "someone who requires more of you than God does." Legalists have a fixed idea about how people should live. In addition to the law of Moses, Pharisees and others had adopted laws passed down by tradition. It was a set of do's and don'ts that were nearly impossible to keep. Jesus refused to abide by the traditions, making him a large target for the Pharisees.

As a rule, Jesus didn't seek confrontation, but he never backed away from it. Many times the Pharisees came to test him, chastise him, or ridicule him. They found Jesus to be a formidable opponent. Despite their best legal minds and those of the scribes, they failed at every attempt to force a false teaching from Jesus. Over time, the tension escalated. People by the thousands began to follow Jesus, undermining the Pharisees' influence and popularity. They were losing their audience.

The Pharisees took to name-calling. In Matthew, they accused Jesus of casting out demons by the power of Beelzebub, the ruler of demons. Jesus' response included the famous line: "Any city or house divided against itself will not stand" (Matthew 12:25 NASB). The attacks persisted.

Jesus preached a message he aimed straight at the Pharisees. He pulled no punches. His words were sharp, direct, and unambiguous. Jesus unloaded on them. The sermon is recorded in Matthew 23.

In the first eight verses, Jesus warns his listeners about the Pharisees, accusing them of hypocrisy, of laying impossible burdens upon the people, and of doing everything for show including making themselves more noticeable by the clothing they wore. Jesus said they loved being called rabbi, sought the "chief seats in the synagogues" (v. 6 NASB), and more. He portrayed them as arrogant egotists who elevated themselves at the expense of others.

Jesus wasn't finished. In Matthew 23:13–36, Jesus took the gloves off and issued eight "woes" to the scribes and Pharisees. Woe to the

- hypocrites who keep people out of heaven.

- hypocrites because they take advantage of widows and yet stand in the street praying as if they were godly men.

- hypocrites who travel far and near to make one convert then make him like them.

- blind men who mislead the people with foolish teaching.

When the Pharisees heard the crowd arguing about Jesus, they got together with the chief priests and sent some temple police to arrest him.

John 7:32 CEV

- hypocrites who focus on the small things while neglecting mercy and faithfulness. He called them "blind guides, who strain out a gnat and swallow a camel!" (v. 24 NASB).

- hypocrites who look good on the outside, but inside they are dirty and self-indulgent.

- hypocrites who are like whitewashed tombs, beautiful on the outside but inside filled with dead men's bones and decay.

- hypocrites who build tombs for the prophets and the righteous men of the past but who would have been on the side of those who killed them. He then calls them serpents and a brood of vipers (v. 33).

Myth Buster

Jesus is often portrayed as meek and mild, and, while that is true, it is incorrect to portray him as weak, withdrawn, and timid. Jesus knew how to stand his ground, how to answer his critics, how to stand up for those who couldn't stand up for themselves. Some people have confused "meek" with "weak." Meekness is not the absence of strength; it is the control of strength. Jesus stood up to his accusers, and he refused to alter his teaching or be diverted from his mission. He spoke plainly and at times fiercely. Jesus should be thought of as a strong figure.

Final Thought

Jesus' life is an example of how we can stand up to opposition, fight for the right, and stand our ground while not descending to the level of our attackers. Wise words are still the best way to silence the critic.

Check Your Understanding

- **Should we be surprised by how direct and harsh Jesus was with the Pharisees?**

Not at all. The image of a milquetoast Jesus doesn't do justice to the truth. Sometimes direct, undiluted truth is the best way to communicate.

- **What else did Jesus achieve by confronting the Pharisees in his "Eight Woes" sermon?**

The listeners learned that they were responsible for their own righteousness and didn't need self-appointed watchdogs to keep them on track. They learned what was wrong with the Pharisees' behavior so they could avoid it. They also learned they could stand up to the legalists themselves.

- **Who is responsible for our spiritual condition?**

We are responsible for our own relationship with God through Jesus Christ. Caring ministers can teach and lead, but we are responsible for our faith decisions. It is therefore important that we know the truth.

Those Who Challenged Jesus—The Saducees

If the Pharisees were the religious conservatives of the day, then the Sadducees were the religious liberals. They were a small group drawn from the priests and the aristocracy of Jerusalem. They rejected the religious beliefs that most of the people held, denying all but the books of Moses as authoritative, and dismissing the oral traditions the Pharisees loved so much. They also denied the existence of angels, future judgments, and any kind of resurrection—the very things Jesus taught were true. Until Jesus came along, the Pharisees and Sadducees were enemies. In Jesus, they found a common cause of hatred.

The Gospels mention the Sadducees fourteen times and never in a positive light. Their first mention occurs when they go to John the Baptist for baptism. John's response was not the warm and fuzzy one they expected. "You brood of vipers, who warned you to flee from the wrath to come?" (Matthew 3:7 NASB). John recognized the false piety of the group and called them on it.

Jesus' opinion was no better. Several times he warned his disciples to "beware of the leaven . . . of the Sadducees" (Matthew 16:6 NASB). Leaven is yeast and used to make dough rise. In Jesus' opinion, a little bit of Sadducee teaching could ruin a great deal of "spiritual bread."

This divided the council—the Pharisees against the Sadducees—for the Sadducees say there is no resurrection or angels or spirits, but the Pharisees believe in all of these.

Acts 23:7–8 NLT

The Pharisees and Sadducees came, and to test Jesus they asked him to show them a sign from heaven.

Matthew 16:1 NRSV

The Sadducees pressed Jesus to perform miracles (Matthew 16:1), something he refused to do on command. They created clever tests for Jesus, including a story about a woman who marries only to have her husband die (Luke 20:27–38). The woman remarries and the same happens again. This repeats seven times. They then asked, "In the resurrection therefore, which one's wife will she be?" (v. 33 NASB). They mistakenly felt this would put an end to Jesus' teaching about the resurrection.

Even after Jesus' death and resurrection, the Sadducees continued to harass the church. The church proclaimed that Jesus had risen from the dead, something the Sadducees had said was impossible. Everything in Jesus' ministry and work ran counter to the Sadducees' beliefs. In the end, the Sadducees disappeared, but Jesus and the church he founded continued.

Final Thought

The Sadducees serve as a graphic example of what happens when a group falls in love with its tradition rather than truth. No matter how much evidence the Sadducees saw, they would not let go of long-held traditions. Truth should never take a backseat to ritual.

Check Your Understanding

- **Why do you suppose the Sadducees were so reluctant to change?**

Human nature, now as then, is to resist change. Change often means admitting our previous errors, and that is difficult for many people. The Sadducees liked things the way they were.

- **Do people resist change today?**

Most do. We are all hampered by emotional inertia—the desire to stay as we are. Change comes with inconvenience. That doesn't make it wrong, but it makes it difficult.

Those Who Tried to Outsmart Jesus—
The Scribes

Professionals have a special standing in our society. One definition describes a professional as someone whose occupation requires a high level of education and specialized training. Doctors, lawyers, architects, and engineers are some of the first professionals who come to mind. They are unique because of the number of years of training required before they can practice. The professionals in Jesus' day were the scribes. Initially, a scribe was someone who wrote or copied documents for a living. Such men were extremely valuable in the ancient world. In Jesus' day, they had been elevated to a high status.

From the beginning, men who could write became invaluable to society. In Jesus' day, scribes were more than people who jotted down notes and events. Because most of their writing and copying dealt with the religious texts, they became experts on the material they penned. The New Testament refers to them as "lawyers," not of civil law, but of biblical law. Their work made them walking reference books.

The message of the cross is foolishness to those who are perishing, but to us who are being saved it is the power of God.

1 Corinthians 1:18 NIV

Consider Him who endured such hostility from sinners against Himself, lest you become weary and discouraged in your souls.

Hebrews 12:3 NKJV

When the wise men came to King Herod looking for the birthplace of Jesus, Herod turned to his "chief priests and scribes" (Matthew 2:4 NKJV) to see where the Messiah was to be born. They quickly cited Micah 5:2, which lists Bethlehem as the birthplace. The scribes were the creators of the synagogue service, a small, local gathering where people could hear the scribes teach.

They had three responsibilities: (1) preserve religious law, (2) teach students, and (3) judge religious disputes. Many became prideful in their positions, requiring reverence from their students that surpassed what the students gave their parents. They wore long robes, uttered lengthy prayers, and sought social preeminence, yet they cared little for the people who turned to them for instruction. Jesus criticized their behavior (Mark 12:38–40).

They turned on Jesus quickly, attempting to trick him. They were part of the group that brought the woman caught in adultery to Jesus to force him to choose between the law of Moses and mercy. Jesus' teaching irritated them beyond reason. They wanted Jesus dead (Matthew 26:3–4). Later, they plagued the early church, challenging the apostles whenever possible.

Final Thought

Jesus polarized the world. Some saw in him truth and salvation; others saw someone who disrupted the status quo. The scribes, Pharisees, and Sadducees chose to resist Jesus at every turn, yet millions upon millions of people through the ages have found Jesus to be trustworthy in everything.

Check Your Understanding

- **Why were religious leaders so resistant to Jesus and his message?**

Their position in society, their income, and their influence were bound to tradition. Jesus brought a change in teaching that threatened the influence of the religious leaders. In short, he was upsetting the apple cart.

- **Why didn't the scribes recognize the truth about Jesus in the Scriptures they taught so frequently?**

Knowing the truth and accepting the truth are very different acts. Some of the religious leaders and scribes did become followers, but they had to be willing to change, and change can be very difficult for some.

The End of the Beginning

Jesus' ultimate destination was Jerusalem and the cross.
The last days of Jesus were torturous and filled with abuse.
Still, he faced it all on our behalf.

Contents

He died for everyone so that those who receive his new life will no longer live for themselves. Instead, they will live for Christ, who died and was raised for them.

2 Corinthians 5:15 NLT

The Triumphal Entry into Jerusalem

Every year the Academy of Motion Picture Arts and Sciences holds the Academy Awards, and every year hundreds of people gather outside the theater so they can have the privilege of seeing a movie star. For some, it is a great joy to see their favorite actor. There's no conversation, just a chance to wave and call the person's name. People like to be around the famous. Jesus experienced such a crowd on his way into Jerusalem. For them it was a joyous time. For Jesus the emotions were different. Jesus was less than a week away from the cross.

✳

When a Roman general was victorious in battle, killing at least five thousand of the enemy, he could expect a Roman triumph ceremony as he returned to his city. He would ride into town on a steed and parade along a line of captured enemies. People would sing his praises. The week before Jesus went to the cross he rode into town and received a similar welcome.

John 12:12–19 and two other Gospels record the events. Jesus rode a donkey up the hill into Jerusalem surrounded by a cheering crowd. People placed palm branches (a symbol of victory) on the path before him and shouted, "Hosanna! Blessed is He who comes in the name of the LORD, even the King of Israel" (v. 13 NASB). Much of this praise came because Jesus had raised Lazarus from the dead, and word had spread.

Your king has won a victory, and he is coming to you. He is humble and rides on a donkey; he comes on the colt of a donkey.

Zechariah 9:9 CEV

O Zion, messenger of good news, shout from the mountaintops! Shout it louder, O Jerusalem. Shout, and do not be afraid. Tell the towns of Judah, "Your God is coming!"

Isaiah 40:9 NLT

Unlike a conquering Roman general, however, Jesus came in humility. He rode a donkey instead of a powerful horse, he brought no captives with him, he wore no crown, and he carried no sword. For the moment, the crowd loved him, but things would change. The same people who called "Hosanna" ("Save us") would soon chant "Crucify him!" (Matthew 27:22 NIV). In the first case, the people hailed him as King; in the second case, they rejected him as a criminal.

In the midst of the hubbub, the praise, and the singing, Jesus continued to Jerusalem to his betrayal, trials, and crucifixion. Victory would be achieved, but it would come at the cost of his life.

Final Thought

 The crowd didn't understand Jesus' purpose or their own need. They wanted a conquering king and got a sacrificial one instead. We don't get to tell Jesus what kind of Savior he is going to be, we accept the kind of Savior he is.

Check Your Understanding

- **Why would the crowd be overjoyed at Jesus' arrival one day, and later turn their backs on him?**

Many factors play a role, but one of the most prominent was that their real need was overshadowed by their felt need. They wanted freedom from the Romans, but what they really needed was freedom from sin and bondage to religious leaders.

- **Jesus never allowed himself to be pressed into a mold made by others. Why?**

Jesus was clear about his mission from the very beginning. He never took his eyes off the goal, which was to bring humankind back into a relationship with God.

The Lord's Supper—Portraying His Own Death

Many years ago, a popular parlor game was charades. People gathered around an open area and watched as one of the guests tried to convey an idea without using words. Based on hand gestures, expressions, and body language, participants would shout out their guesses as to what the play meant. Jesus gave the church two ordinances—religious ceremonies—to be practiced until he returned. Both are symbolic and involve the worshipper in an action that reminds all in attendance of the first time the act was performed. One such ordinance is the Lord's Supper, called the Eucharist in some denominations.

In the upper room, just hours before Jesus' betrayal and arrest, he instituted a practice that Christians have repeated to this day. Jesus was celebrating the Feast of Passover when he broke from tradition and used two of the elements to portray what he would endure in the hours ahead.

On the table rested wine and unleavened bread. Jesus took the bread, broke it, and called it his body. He took a cup of wine and declared it his blood of the covenant shed for many (Mark 14:22–31) and passed it among his disciples. As he shared the bread and wine, he commanded the disciples to do this in remembrance of him (Luke 22:19). Christians have been doing so ever since.

I received from the Lord what I also handed on to you, that the Lord Jesus on the night when he was betrayed took a loaf of bread, and when he had given thanks, he broke it and said, "This is my body that is for you. Do this in remembrance of me." In the same way he took the cup also, after supper, saying, "This cup is the new covenant in my blood. Do this, as often as you drink it, in remembrance of me." For as often as you eat this bread and drink the cup, you proclaim the Lord's death until he comes.

1 Corinthians 11:23–26 NRSV

While breaking the bread and passing the cup are simple, the message behind the acts is startling. In a sense, Jesus was attending his own wake. The emotion in the room was thick, and the weight of the future and the world settled heavily on Jesus' shoulders. He began the ceremony with, "I have earnestly desired to eat this Passover with you before I suffer" (Luke 22:15 NASB). Jesus stood on the threshold of events that would inflict more pain than could be imagined. He poured out his heart the way he poured out the wine.

As ugly as the arrest, trials, torture, and crucifixion were, they are central to Christianity. Jesus came to die for humankind, to sacrifice himself for others.

Take It to Heart

Denominations celebrate the Lord's Supper differently and at different intervals, but they do so for the same reasons: first, because Jesus commanded his followers to do so; and second, because it reminds them of the sacrifice Jesus made. To partake in the Lord's Supper is to align ourselves with the death of Jesus.

Check Your Understanding

- **Admittedly, Jesus' portraying his death seems odd. Why would he do that?**

Jesus' death on the cross and his resurrection are the foundation of the Christian faith. His was no ordinary death, but one that reconciled the people with God and, consequently, should be remembered.

- **Jesus included his disciples in the symbolic act. Why?**

Because they, like all people, were the beneficiaries of Jesus' sacrificial death. By communing with Jesus' death, they were aligning with him and all he taught.

Alone in the Garden of Gethsemane

One of the most familiar paintings of Jesus is Heinrich Hofmann's portrayal of Jesus in the garden of Gethsemane. It shows a robe-clad Jesus kneeling at a flat rock and gazing skyward in prayer. It's a lovely, serene painting, but it misses the point. Jesus' time in the garden of Gethsemane was anything but serene. It was rough, emotional, and physically brutal. The Gospels show a heartrending scene of Jesus in anxious, soul-twisting prayer. Before him waited an agony beyond words. Not just physical, but spiritual as well. Matthew, Mark, and Luke give us the details.

Outside Jerusalem was (and is) an olive grove, a private garden to which Jesus had access. It must have been a beautiful place, populated with olive trees and other plants. It was the kind of place one went to relax. Ironically, relaxation was the furthest thing from Jesus' mind. We don't know who owned the garden, but after celebrating Passover and delivering his final teaching to the disciples, Jesus went to the site.

> Going a little farther, he fell with his face to the ground and prayed, "My Father, if it is possible, may this cup be taken from me. Yet not as I will, but as you will."
>
> Matthew 26:39 NIV
>
> Ought not the Christ to have suffered these things and to enter into His glory?
>
> Luke 24:26 NKJV

When he entered the garden, he left behind all but three of his disciples. He then went on a short distance alone. No crowds attended him, and only three of his closest friends were in sight. There, in the dark Jerusalem night, the world fell on Jesus. The word *Gethsemane* means "oil press." An oil press was used to squeeze oil from the olive. It's symbolic of what Jesus would go through that night.

Soul-shredding emotions rolled over Jesus like a tsunami. The words used in the Gospels give us a hint at how severe the experience was: *distress*, *agony*, *horrified*, *heavy*, and *distraught*. Emotions are powerful things. The word *emotion* means "movement within." An emotion is something felt physically. It begins mentally but is always expressed physically. When we're angry, our blood pressure rises and our muscles tense. When we're depressed, our shoulders slump, we tend to gaze down, and we feel heaviness in our chests. The emotions Jesus experienced had a profound physical effect on him.

How crushing were those emotions? They forced him to the ground. Jesus walked a short distance from the three disciples, and then the emotional tonnage drove him to the ground. He rose only to stagger a few more steps and then collapse to the cold ground again.

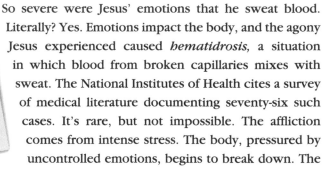

So severe were Jesus' emotions that he sweat blood. Literally? Yes. Emotions impact the body, and the agony Jesus experienced caused *hematidrosis,* a situation in which blood from broken capillaries mixes with sweat. The National Institutes of Health cites a survey of medical literature documenting seventy-six such cases. It's rare, but not impossible. The affliction comes from intense stress. The body, pressured by uncontrolled emotions, begins to break down. The phrase "I'm sweating blood" comes from Jesus' experience in the garden of Gethsemane.

If we stitch together the accounts given by Matthew and Mark, and if we set aside the grammar rules about redundancy, we get an awkward but revealing narration of Jesus' experience: "They came to a place named Gethsemane, and he told his disciples, 'Sit here while I pray.' He took Peter, James, and John with him, and he was overwhelmed with *deep distress, amazement, alarm,* and *was horrified, heavy, uncomfortable, unfamiliar,* and *distraught.* 'My soul is so surrounded with grief that I am close to dying.'"

Words are powerful things, but they fail in certain circumstances. What Jesus endured cannot be revealed with just words. Our imagination must take us further. Jesus laid bare his soul when he said the grief and sorrow was so great it was close to killing him. That isn't hyperbole. Jesus came close to dying in that garden.

What caused Jesus such distress? Was it the knowledge that he would be betrayed, arrested, and crucified over the next few hours? Certainly it was that. Who could face such a situation and not be shaken to the core? But it was more than that—it was the weight of the world's sin. The apostle Paul made a provocative statement in his letter to the Corinthian church: "He made Him who knew no sin to be sin for us, that we might become the righteousness of God in Him" (2 Corinthians 5:21 NKJV). The perfect took on the punishment due the imperfect. All the guilt, pain, regret, and sorrow came to rest upon him. Jesus went to the cross for humanity, and he had to pass through the garden of Gethsemane to do it.

> He said to them, "I have eagerly desired to eat this Passover with you before I suffer; for I tell you, I will not eat it until it is fulfilled in the kingdom of God."
>
> Luke 22:15–16 NRSV

Myth Buster

Psychiatrists sometimes deal with individuals who display a Christ complex. For some, the condition manifests as an air of superiority or entitlement; for others it is an overwhelming desire to sacrifice themselves for others. Jesus didn't suffer from a Christ complex. He didn't long for the torture of the cross. He agonized over it until he sweat blood. He even prayed for things to change. In the end, however, he went to the cross willingly because his love for us was greater than his fear. The agony began long before the cross.

Final Thought

 The saddest element is that Jesus endured it alone. He brought three of his disciples to watch and pray for him, but the biblical account states they fell asleep—three times. Jesus' closest disciples couldn't stay awake when he needed them. Jesus went through the agony while his friends slept.

Check Your Understanding

- **Does seeing Jesus wrestle with fear and other emotions diminish him?**

Not at all. There is no sin in experiencing and struggling with emotions. Jesus was about to go through what no man has ever experienced— not just death, but dying with the weight of the world's sin on his shoulders. That may have been the most painful thing of all.

- **The Gospel accounts show a very different Jesus after his time in Gethsemane. What is different?**

The agonizing prayer ended, and Jesus rose from the ground to face the mob that came to arrest him. He went through his arrest, trials, and crucifixion with courage and commitment.

- **The one who had ministered to the needs of thousands went through his turmoil alone. Had the three disciples stayed awake and comforted Jesus, would it have changed things?**

No. Their presence would have shown great love and commitment, but Jesus would have passed through the same suffering anyway. It was an unavoidable agony.

Jesus' Unanswered Prayer

Abraham Lincoln's Gettysburg Address is one of the best speeches ever written—and one of the shortest. Just 238 words long, the speech continues to move readers today. Edward Everett spoke before Lincoln and took two hours to deliver his message. Lincoln took closer to two minutes. No one remembers Everett's speech, but nearly every American knows of Lincoln's. The New Testament records several of Jesus' prayers, and they are wonderful to read. In the upper room, he uttered a long prayer that has been studied in detail. Still, Jesus' most famous prayer is short, poignant, and moving.

Just twenty-one words: "Abba, Father, . . . everything is possible for you. Take this cup from me. Yet not what I will, but what you will" (Mark 14:36 NIV).

He uttered the prayer with urgency. The words passed from the lips of Jesus as he suffered in the garden of Gethsemane. His first words are those of a son to a father: "Abba" and "Father." *Abba* is the Aramaic word for "father." *Abba* is the familiar word a child would use to address his dad. *Father* carries a little more formality. This is a personal prayer.

He said to them, "I am so sad that I feel as if I am dying. Stay here and keep awake with me."

Matthew 26:38 CEV

"Everything is possible for you." Jesus was doing more than making a theological statement; he was setting up his request. He prayed as many of us do in times of crisis. "You can do anything; will you do this?"

While he lived on earth, anticipating death, Jesus cried out in pain and wept in sorrow as he offered up priestly prayers to God.

Hebrews 5:7 MSG

"Take this cup from me." What cup? The cup of pending suffering. He was referring to the horrible events that would begin in the hours ahead. Submerged in dark emotions we can only imagine, Jesus asked for a way out. But he didn't stop there.

The rest of the prayer reveals Jesus' heart. He prayed that God's will would be done, not his own, and if that meant going to the cross, then to the cross he would go. Jesus did go to the cross, so in a sense a part of his prayer was rejected. The cup would not pass. But the rest of the prayer—"not My will, but Yours, be done" (Luke 22:42 NKJV)—was honored.

Take It to Heart

Jesus willingly carried the weight of the world's sin on his back. The degree of pre-arrest suffering is demonstrated in his request to "let this cup pass from Me" (Matthew 26:39 NASB). The rest of the prayer shows Jesus' love and determination: "Yet not as I will, but as You will" (v. 39 NASB).

Check Your Understanding

- **Does Jesus' prayer in the garden of Gethsemane show weakness?**

There is nothing weak about Jesus. Just going to Gethsemane was a heroic act. The suffering he experienced there far outstripped what most of us will ever experience. The prayer was an honest expression of how he felt, but it also revealed his commitment to go forward.

- **What does Jesus' prayer teach us about our own Gethsemane moments?**

Go to God in prayer; be honest; be specific; be obedient. Jesus never treated God like a vending machine of help, but as the One to whom we should all be submissive.

Jesus on Trial

One of the most popular types of shows on television is the legal drama. From the days of Perry Mason to *Law and Order* to the comedy *Boston Legal,* we love legal shows. There's something about seeing the evil convicted and the innocent set free. In real life, the opposite sometimes happens. In Jesus' case, he faced not one mock trial but four. The victim of a conspiracy, Jesus was handed from leader to leader for judgment before being sent to the cross. The man of ultimate innocence was tried by men mired in guilt.

✽

Jesus stood before Jewish and Roman courts in four trials.

Trial 1. Jesus' first trial took place in the home of Annas, the former high priest (Luke 22:54). Rome had deposed Annas in AD 15, but he remained influential. Annas pushed Jesus for information about his teaching, but Jesus refused to cooperate. Instead, Jesus suggested the old man talk to people who had heard his sermons. One of the temple police struck Jesus for the comment. Before long, men were taking turns striking Jesus. Annas sent Jesus to Caiaphas. Caiaphas assembled the Sanhedrin, the Jewish court. They also beat Jesus.

Trial 2. This one took place before the local Roman governor, Pontius Pilate. Jesus' enemies had a problem: they wanted him dead, but only a

"You are a king, then!" said Pilate. Jesus answered, "You are right in saying I am a king. In fact, for this reason I was born, and for this I came into the world, to testify to the truth. Everyone on the side of truth listens to me." "What is truth?" Pilate asked. With this, he went out again to the Jews and said, "I find no basis for a charge against him. But it is your custom for me to release to you one prisoner at the time of the Passover. Do you want me to release 'the king of the Jews'?" They shouted back, "No, not him! Give us Barabbas!" Now Barabbas had taken part in a rebellion.

John 18:37–40 NIV

Roman official could call for an execution. They needed Pilate to sign on. It was an odd pairing since Pilate hated Jews. Still, the religious leaders needed his help and accused Jesus of a crime that would get Pilate's attention—declaring himself king, a capital offense.

Trial 3. Pilate sent Jesus to Herod Antipas, a Jewish leader from Jesus' area. Since it was Passover time, Herod Antipas was in Jerusalem. There Jesus endured more beatings and mockery before being sent back to Pilate.

Trial 4. Again, Jesus stood before Pilate, who could find no crime. The governor had a habit of releasing one prisoner during Passover, so he offered Jesus or Barabbas, a criminal. The people chose Barabbas. Pilate literally washed his hands of the matter. Jesus would soon be crucified.

Final Thought

Few people living in free countries would condone brutality before or even after conviction. Jesus knew the treatment he would experience, the rejection he would receive, and yet he was willing to endure it to complete a mission that opened the gates of eternity for us.

Check Your Understanding

- **One thing we notice when we study the trials of Jesus is that none of his enemies or judges could find fault with him. Why?**

Jesus was an innocent, a victim of conspiracy, hatred, and a corrupt system of justice. Since Jesus had committed no religious or social crime, his accusers had to lie.

- **Reading the Gospel accounts reveals that Jesus went through all the stages of trial alone. No one stood up for him or beside him. Why?**

Fear. It was a horrible thing to be a Jew on trial in a Roman system. It was equally horrifying to be judged by the religious leaders of the day. Jesus walked that path alone.

The Barabbas Mystery

A drama played out in the Antonia Fortress, a large building next to the temple where Jesus was most likely tried and flogged. It's a familiar story and on the surface seems a simple one, but a closer look reveals layers of mystery and irony. Jesus' enemies took him captive, abused and ridiculed him, but were prevented by law from executing him, so they took him to Pontius Pilate and demanded Jesus be tried. They had everything figured out. What they couldn't have anticipated was the story being told just below the surface.

The world is filled with the famous and the infamous. Barabbas has a single claim to fame: he was a convicted criminal who was due to be executed but was set free. Barabbas is mentioned by name in all four Gospels and described as an insurrectionist (Mark 15:7), a thief (John 18:40), a murderer (Mark 15:7), and a notorious man (Matthew 27:16). Not flattering terms. He was not the kind of man anyone wanted for a neighbor. The Roman authorities had arrested him and condemned him to death. For all Barabbas knew, this was to be his last few hours alive. But then things turned interesting. Roman guards led Barabbas, no doubt beaten, to Pilate. He would have seen Jesus there, battered, spat upon, and bound. What Barabbas couldn't know was the role he'd

I will give him the honors of a victorious soldier, because he exposed himself to death. He was counted among the rebels. He bore the sins of many and interceded for rebels.

Isaiah 53:12 NLT

I tell you, this scripture must be fulfilled in me, "And he was counted among the lawless"; and indeed what is written about me is being fulfilled.

Luke 22:37 NRSV

play over the next few minutes and the concepts he'd come to represent. Barabbas and Jesus are bound together by points of interest.

The first thing to notice is his name: Barabbas. *Barabbas* is a compound word combining *bar* and *Abba*. *Bar* means "son of," such as the Jewish celebration of Bar Mitzvah, which means "Son of the Law." *Abba* is an Aramaic word meaning "father." Barabbas (Bar Abba) means "Son of the Father." Here is where the paradox begins. Jesus often referred to himself as the Son of God. In those awful hours, Jesus stood side by side with a man named "Son of the Father."

There's more about the name. Several ancient versions of the Gospels include a first name for Barabbas: Jesus. If these documents are correct, then Jesus the Son of God stood next to Jesus Son of the Father. If that's all the parallelism there is, then we might have an interesting coincidence, but there is more.

Barabbas had been convicted of insurrection, a crime requiring death. The charge against Jesus was that he claimed to be a king—in other words, insurrection. It is the charge that got him crucified. Here things turn poignant. Jesus would be nailed to a cross. That cross had been prepared for Barabbas. Jesus would die on Barabbas's cross.

Another odd observation has to do with guilt and innocence. Barabbas was a notorious man, a thief and a killer. Jesus was a famous man innocent of any crime. Yet because the crowd, who had been stirred up by the religious leaders, called for the release of Barabbas, Jesus was condemned.

Barabbas took the lives of others; Jesus *gave* his life for others. Barabbas was motivated by hatred for the Romans; Jesus was motivated by love for everyone. Barabbas was freed by the crowd; Jesus died for the crowd. Jesus is the most famous person ever; Barabbas disappeared forever, remembered only because of this passage.

The story of Barabbas is a living parable, a historical event that carries a message. Barabbas represented the "every person." Jesus literally and metaphorically took Barabbas's place on the cross, and in so doing he died not only for Barabbas but also for those who conspired against him and the crowd that sold him out. Barabbas represents us. We might not

> Pilate asked them, "Do you want me to free the king of the Jews?" Pilate knew that the chief priests had brought Jesus to him because they were jealous. But the chief priests told the crowd to ask Pilate to free Barabbas.
>
> Mark 15:9–11 CEV

be notorious murderers, thieves, or insurrectionists, but we still need a Savior.

At the time, Jesus was the only one who could see the connections. He would go to the cross with no one fully knowing the sacrifice he was making for humanity. Years later, the apostle Paul would write to a church in Rome, "Very rarely will anyone die for a righteous man, though for a good man someone might possibly dare to die. But God demonstrates his own love for us in this: While we were still sinners, Christ died for us" (Romans 5:7–8 NIV). Jesus died for the world, including Jesus Bar Abbas.

Myth Buster

Some assume that Christianity is only for good people. Christianity is for everyone. It is a faith that helps people change. It starts where they are and helps move them closer to Jesus. The history of Christianity shows that it is more hospital than hotel. Church isn't designed for perfect people; it's designed for imperfect people looking for a new life. The first leader of the church was Peter, and he denied Jesus three times, swearing he never knew him. Yet he went on to change the world. Christianity has a place for everyone. Jesus saw to that.

Final Thought

Barabbas represents us: people who need forgiveness and an extra chance at life, people who long to have their pasts forgotten so they can face tomorrow with a clean slate. Had it not been for Jesus, Barabbas would have died, but Jesus became his substitute. He was everyone's substitute.

Check Your Understanding

• **Are parallels and contrasts between Jesus and Barabbas a coincidence?**

Bible students agree that coincidence has nothing to do with the Bible. The parallels between Barabbas and Jesus are, in a sense, a parable not told but lived. That parable teaches a great deal about Jesus and his ministry.

• **In what ways does Barabbas represent us as individuals?**

Barabbas represents everyone. He was a man, guilty of many things, who needed to be saved from his situation and condition. Because of Jesus' sacrifice, Barabbas got a second, life-changing chance, the same chance Jesus gives to us all.

• **The story of Barabbas is a silent sermon. What is the core message of that sermon?**

Jesus the innocent died for the guilty. Barabbas didn't deserve freedom, and yet he was given it nonetheless. The New Testament teaches that everyone needs Jesus.

The Death Jesus Died

Death is difficult to face. Doctors, nurses, ministers, firefighters, police, and others learn to face it, but even for them, death is heartrending. To understand Jesus requires understanding his death. There's an urge to skip over this part of the story, to look away from the garish brutality he experienced, but to do so is to miss the center of his work. Throughout his ministry, Jesus brought healing and relief from illness. At the end of his ministry, he endured pain beyond imagination. Without his death, we would have Jesus the Great Teacher, but we would not have Jesus the Savior.

✳

After his trials, Roman soldiers flogged Jesus. Flogging was done with a cat-o'-nine-tails, a whip of multiple strands weighted with metal at the ends. Jesus would have been stripped, tied to a post with his hands over his head so he couldn't fall, and then a soldier would have begun to whip him. A Roman could receive only thirty-nine lashes. There was no limit for Jews. Many condemned men died from the beating.

The word *excruciating* comes from the Latin and means "out of the cross." When we speak of excruciating pain, we mean crucifixion-like pain. Execution by crucifixion began with the Persians, but the Romans took it to new heights. There were several ways of crucifying and several styles of crosses.

The Father loves me, because I give up my life, so that I may receive it back again. No one takes my life from me. I give it up willingly! I have the power to give it up and the power to receive it back again, just as my Father commanded me to do.

John 10:17–18 CEV

Although he was crucified in weakness, he now lives by the power of God. We, too, are weak, just as Christ was, but when we deal with you we will be alive with him and will have God's power.

2 Corinthians 3:4 NLT

Bible scholars believe Jesus was hanged on a cross that resembled a small "t." Most likely the crossbeam was dropped to the ground, Jesus was forced to lie on it, and then square iron nails were driven through his hands. It is likely that his wrists were tied to the bcam to keep him from pulling free. The beam would have been raised and attached to the vertical piece of the cross. A square spike was probably driven through his feet. Sometimes the executioners put the condemned person's feet on either side of the upright and drove spikes through the ankles.

Death came slowly. Shock, blood loss, and exposure contributed to the crucified person's death. Many medical specialists think the real cause of death was suffocation, which occurred when the crucified individual became too weak to breathe.

Myth Buster

 If we read the crucifixion accounts closely, it appears that Jesus chose the moment of his death (Luke 23:46). Jesus spoke of his death when he said, "No one takes [my life] from me, but I lay it down of my own accord" (John 10:18 NIV). It is likely that Jesus completed his mission and simply let himself die.

Check Your Understanding

- **Jesus was not the only person to die on a cross. Rome crucified hundreds, maybe thousands, of people. What makes his crucifixion so different?**

The means of death is secondary to the one who died. Had Jesus been stoned to death, as was the Jewish custom, the meaning would be the same. God came in the flesh to die so we could live.

- **Many people shy away from Jesus on the cross, preferring to focus on Jesus the teacher. Is this a good idea?**

It's easy to understand why people do this. Crucifixion is ugly and disturbing, but it is, nonetheless, a part of Jesus' work. To fully appreciate Jesus, we must see all that he did—including the cross.

Buried in a Tomb

In the Western world, people let professionals take care of burial matters. In most cases, after a person dies, the family doesn't see the body again until the viewing or funeral, and then only if the service is "open casket." Things worked differently in Jesus' time. Family members handled all aspects of burials. Joseph of Arimathea and Nicodemus, ranking Jewish leaders, took charge of Jesus' body. Joseph did one other thing: he provided his family tomb. Providing the tomb was as much an act of love as preparing the body. That tomb would become the most famous crypt in history.

Jesus was laid in a borrowed tomb. Today, tens of thousands of people travel to Israel to visit what is assumed to be Jesus' tomb. No one can be certain which tomb Jesus was buried in, only that it once belonged to Joseph of Arimathea and was close to Jerusalem.

Tombs came in two types, natural cave openings and hand-hewed. The latter were expensive, and only the well-to-do could afford them. Joseph of Arimathea was one of those. After Joseph and Nicodemus prepared the body, they or their servants most likely carried Jesus on a wood stretcher to the tomb. There they laid him on a stone bier or in a niche carved into one of the walls. Some tombs had two chambers. The first was an inner chamber where the dead rested until the process of decomposition was completed. (Jews didn't embalm their dead.) Afterward the bones of the

> He was assigned a grave with the wicked, and with the rich in his death, though he had done no violence, nor was any deceit in his mouth.
>
> Isaiah 53:9 NIV

> To these He also presented Himself alive after His suffering, by many convincing proofs, appearing to them over a period of forty days and speaking of the things concerning the kingdom of God.
>
> Acts 1:3 NASB

deceased were gathered and placed in a limestone ossuary, a receptacle for holding bones. The ossuary would be stored in an outer chamber. Since the tomb was new, Jesus was the only occupant.

The last thing the men (we assume Mary was present) did was to roll a large stone in front of the tomb's opening. The stone looked like a large rock wheel and would have been set on a small incline. The incline would make moving the stone into place easier and removing it more difficult. This stone "door" sealed the tomb, keeping out scavengers.

For three days, all eternity pivoted on that borrowed tomb.

Myth Buster

 Detractors claim the disciples stole the body of Jesus to fabricate a resurrection. Jesus' enemies convinced Pilate to provide guards and seal the tomb (Matthew 27:62-66). Scholars believe Pilate's men stretched a cord over the stone and sealed it to the side with wax. Breaking the seal was inviting a death sentence.

Check Your Understanding

- **What dangers did Nicodemus and Joseph of Arimathea face in taking the initiative in burying Jesus?**

They were aligning themselves with a man arraigned by Jesus' enemies and convicted by the Roman system. Many of Jesus' enemies were men they met with frequently. The act may have destroyed their careers.

- **There are some interesting parallels between Jesus' birth and burial. Can you name some?**

Here are a few: Mary gave birth in a cave; Jesus was laid in a tomb. As an infant, Jesus was laid in a manger (a stone feeding trough); in death he was laid on a stone bier. As a newborn, Jesus was wrapped in swaddling clothes; in death he was wrapped in linens. Mary, his mother, was at his birth and death.

The First Easter—Resurrection

According to CNN, Bryan Berg set a new world's record for card stacking. While some people can create a house of cards, Berg creates skyscrapers of cards, including one that reached the height of 25 feet 9-7/16 inches. No matter how tall the house of cards, it can all tumble down with a gust of wind. Without the resurrection, Christianity is a house of cards. The apostle Paul wrote in 1 Corinthians 15:14, "If Christ has not been raised, our preaching is useless and so is your faith" (NIV). All Christian belief rests on the resurrection of Jesus.

Theologian Albert Mohler Jr. wrote, "The literal, historical, bodily resurrection of Jesus from the dead is the vindication of Jesus' saving work on the cross. The issue is simple—no resurrection, no Christianity."

Five times during his ministry, Jesus predicted he would be arrested, killed, and later resurrected. All the early persecutors of the church had to do to stop Christianity in its tracks was produce the body of Jesus.

Jesus rose from the dead bodily. He ate, and he was seen, touched, spoken to, and recognized by those who saw him die. Twelve times Jesus appeared to his followers. It's interesting to note that Jesus never appeared to his enemies. He made twelve appearances, to as few as one and to as many as five hundred. Although before his death he taught of his resurrection, most of his

> If we died with Christ, we believe that we shall also live with Him, knowing that Christ, having been raised from the dead, dies no more. Death no longer has dominion over Him.
>
> Romans 6:8–9 NKJV
>
> When I saw him, I fell at his feet as though dead. But he placed his right hand on me, saying, "Do not be afraid; I am the first and the last, and the living one. I was dead, and see, I am alive forever and ever; and I have the keys of Death and of Hades."
>
> Revelation 1:17–18 NRSV

followers didn't believe. Several times they doubted his resurrection—until he appeared before them.

Jesus' resurrection was physical, and he made a point of proving it. Mary Magdalene was the first to see him after his burial, and she clung to his feet to such a degree he had to command her to let go (John 20:17). When he appeared to his disciples in the closed upper room he told Thomas, who doubted the resurrection, to put his fingers in the nail holes in his hands and place his hand in the spear wound in his side (John 20:26–29). Thomas fell to his knees and said, "My Lord and my God!" (v. 28 NKJV). For Thomas, seeing was believing.

Final Thought

Jesus' resurrection authenticated his claims of deity and his right to be called Messiah. After Thomas's proclamation of faith, Jesus said, "Because you have seen Me, have you believed? Blessed are they who did not see, and yet believed" (John 20:29 NASB). Today Christians rest their faith in Jesus and on his resurrection.

Check Your Understanding

- **The resurrection of Jesus remains controversial today. Why?**

The resurrection of Jesus was and is unique. It goes against human experience. Still, it is true and remains the miracle that changed the world.

- **Why do you suppose Jesus appeared to followers only after his resurrection?**

The ministry of Jesus would be transferred to his followers. His disciples would travel the known world spreading the gospel. They needed the proof and encouragement that Jesus' resurrection could bring. It gave them confidence and completed the gospel message.

The Lesson of Angels at the Tomb

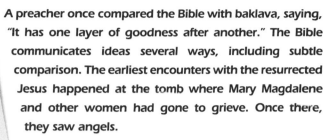

A preacher once compared the Bible with baklava, saying, "It has one layer of goodness after another." The Bible communicates ideas several ways, including subtle comparison. The earliest encounters with the resurrected Jesus happened at the tomb where Mary Magdalene and other women had gone to grieve. Once there, they saw angels.

The resurrection is recorded in all four Gospels, but each reveals different details. Taken together, the accounts mention six angels in or at the tomb after the resurrection. If we imagine a two-chamber tomb and place the angels according to the Gospel descriptions, we can see an interesting pattern.

At the back of the tomb, where Jesus' body had rested, Mary Magdalene saw two angels sitting, one at the head and one at the foot of the bench where the body of Jesus had been lying (John 20:11–12). Luke 24:4 mentions two "men" in dazzling clothing appearing inside the tomb. Mark 16:5 identifies a "young man" in a white robe. Matthew 28:2 shows an angel sitting on the stone that had sealed the tomb. What does it mean?

Not far away stood the temple and its surrounding complex. The temple was the center of Jewish life.

> He himself is the sacrifice that atones for our sins— and not only our sins but the sins of all the world.
>
> 1 John 2:2 NLT

> Behind the curtain was the most holy place. The gold altar that was used for burning incense was in this holy place. The gold-covered sacred chest was also there, and inside it were three things. First, there was a gold jar filled with manna. Then there was Aaron's walking stick that sprouted. Finally, there were the flat stones with the Ten Commandments written on them. On top of the chest were the glorious creatures with wings opened out above the place of mercy.
>
> Hebrews 9:3–5 CEV

The large building had two primary areas into which only priests could go. The Holy of Holies was restricted to the high priest, who entered the room only once a year to make atonement for the nation's sins. Inside the room were two large statues of angels with wings that reached from wall to wall. At one time, they overshadowed the ark of the covenant, a gold box upon which the high priest sprinkled blood from an animal sacrifice. On the lid of the ark were two angels.

There is a parallel between the tomb of Jesus and the Holy of Holies, indicating that Jesus was the sacrifice for the world.

Final Thought

 As the blood of the animal sacrifice was sprinkled between the two angels on the ark of the covenant, so Jesus' blood is the sacrifice for humanity's sin. The tomb became the Holy of Holies; Jesus became the sacrifice; and the angels in the tomb reflected the angelic statues in the temple.

Check Your Understanding

- **Symbolism, like the appearance of the angels in the tomb, plays an important part in biblical revelation. Why choose such an indirect approach?**

The Bible uses several means of getting the truth across, including symbolism. Symbolism engages the reader, causing him or her to dig deeper and remember the truth longer. A symbolic act is more than a clever twist in teaching; it is a powerful way of communicating.

- **Do you think the first people at the empty tomb understood the symbolism?**

Perhaps not at first. Their minds and hearts were caught up in the horrible crucifixion they had seen a few days earlier and the fact that they now faced an empty tomb. It may have taken some time for them and those who followed to put the pieces together.

The Twelve Resurrection Appearances of Jesus

Lord Lyndhurst was one the great legal minds in nineteenth-century England. He said, "I know pretty well what evidence is; and, I tell you, such evidence as that for the resurrection has never broken down yet." The resurrection is the doctrine that holds up the whole church and Christian belief. Without it, everything tumbles to the ground. The resurrection has endured countless attacks over the last two thousand years, and yet it remains unassailable. One reason that this is true is eyewitness testimony. The New Testament gives twelve accounts of Jesus' appearing after his death and burial.

✳

Mary Magdalene. Mary was the first to see Jesus alive again (John 20:11-18). She had gone to the tomb early Sunday morning to grieve and attend to the body. Considering the social constraints of the day, it's fascinating to note the first witness to the resurrection was a woman.

The other women. The second sighting is by a group of women who had gone to the tomb (Matthew 28:8-10). An angel sent them out with a message, but before they got very far, they ran into Jesus. They dropped to the ground, took hold of his feet, and worshipped. Jesus gave them a message for the disciples.

Peter's secret meeting. Peter was the boldest of the disciples and the quickest to speak—something that

In three days God had him up, alive, and out where he could be seen. Not everyone saw him—he wasn't put on public display. Witnesses had been carefully handpicked by God beforehand—us! We were the ones, there to eat and drink with him after he came back from the dead.

Acts 10:40–41 MSG

God raised him from the dead; and for many days he appeared to those who came up with him from Galilee to Jerusalem, and they are now his witnesses to the people.

Acts 13:30–31 NRSV

caused him trouble from time to time. The resurrected Jesus appeared to Peter, but we have almost no information about the event. Paul mentions it in 1 Corinthians 15:5, writing, "He appeared to Cephas" (NASB). Cephas was Peter's Aramaic name. After Jesus' arrest, Peter denied Jesus three times. Jesus and Peter had some things to work out. Luke 24:34 is another reference to Jesus' appearance to Peter.

Two on the road. This is one of the longest accounts of a resurrection appearance. Two disciples were walking the seven miles from Jerusalem to Emmaus (Luke 24:13-35). They passed the time by talking about the crucifixion and rumors of a resurrection. Jesus approached and joined them on the journey. They invited him to dinner, where they came to recognize him. Jesus then disappeared.

The upper room ten. The days after the crucifixion were frightening ones. The disciples spent their time in the upper room behind a locked door. Jesus appeared in their midst (Luke 24:36-49). To prove that he had risen bodily from the grave, he ate fish with them.

The upper room eleven. Jesus again appeared in the upper room, but this time the focus was on Thomas (John 20:24-29). Thomas had missed the first appearance of Jesus and had told the others he wouldn't believe until he could put his finger in the nail holes of Jesus' hands and thrust his hand into the spear wound in Jesus' side. Jesus gave him that opportunity. Thomas dropped to his knees and said, "My Lord and my God!" (v. 28 NASB).

On the mountaintop. At an unnamed mountain in Galilee, Jesus appeared to his disciples again, and there he gave them the Great Commission, marching orders to go into the world teaching and baptizing (Matthew 28:16-20).

The five hundred on the mountaintop. The apostle Paul again included an appearance that isn't recorded elsewhere. We have very little information about this event other than that it occurred on the same mountain in Galilee where Jesus met his disciples and it included more than "five hundred of the brothers at the same time" (1 Corinthians 15:6 NIV).

The seven by the sea. In one of the most remarkable recorded appearances, Jesus showed up on the shore of the Sea of Galilee where Peter and some other disciples were fishing from a boat (John 21:1-14). Jesus repeated a miracle he had worked earlier in his ministry. He then shared a breakfast of fish with those seven disciples.

> What I received I passed on to you as of first importance: that Christ died for our sins according to the Scriptures, that he was buried, that he was raised on the third day according to the Scriptures, and that he appeared to Peter, and then to the Twelve. After that, he appeared to more than five hundred of the brothers at the same time, most of whom are still living, though some have fallen asleep. Then he appeared to James, then to all the apostles, and last of all he appeared to me also, as to one abnormally born.
>
> 1 Corinthians 15:3–8 NIV

James. Again, Paul gave us a detail not found anywhere else. Jesus appeared to James (1 Corinthians 15:7). That's all we know. It was a visit, and nothing else is shared. James, however, would go on to lead the church in Jerusalem after Peter.

At the ascension. Jesus ascended to heaven from a place not far from Jerusalem. He gave his disciples a missionary strategy, then he rose bodily into the sky and out of sight (Luke 24:50-53).

Paul the apostle. Paul became a believer long after the preceding events, but nonetheless he saw Jesus in a shocking way while on the road to Damascus. He planned to persecute the church there (Acts 9:1-9). It's the only instance we know of where Jesus appeared to an enemy.

Myth Buster

Since the first century, there have been those who look back over the years and say, "I know what really happened." Nonsensical ideas have been put forward, ideas that require a greater leap in logic than simply

believing the people who were there. Some have said that Jesus merely swooned but didn't die, or that the Romans became confused and cruci fied the wrong man, or that there was a Jesus double who took his place. Solid scholarship shows such ideas as nonsense. The best interpretation of the data says Jesus rose from the dead and appeared to more than five hundred people over a period of forty days.

Final Thought

 The appearances of Jesus were real events that had profound effects on the witnesses. It turned their sorrow and depression into joy and zeal. His appearances sent men and women into the world testifying to what they had seen and experienced.

Check Your Understanding

- **To whom did Jesus appear after his resurrection?**

In some cases he appeared to individuals (Mary Magdalene, Peter, and James); other times he appeared to small groups (the women at the tomb, the two travelers on their way to Emmaus, and the seven fishing disciples); larger groups (ten disciples then eleven disciples); and a large group of more than five hundred men.

- **What does it mean that Jesus first appeared to Mary Magdalene?**

It could mean several things. It might be nothing more than that she was the first to visit the tomb after the resurrection. It could be that Jesus knew Mary would be willing to believe more easily than others would. Or it could be that Jesus was making a statement about how all-inclusive his ministry was.

Jesus' Ascension into Heaven

The most remarkable exit took place in the village of Bethany just two miles outside Jerusalem. In full view of his disciples, Jesus left this earth—literally. In an act that defied physics and disregarded gravity, Jesus was lifted skyward until he disappeared from sight. It is difficult to imagine something as stunning as the resurrection, but this comes close. Jesus arrived as a baby, born in an obscure town to common people. His environment was unfit for humans, and Mary laid him to rest in a feeding trough. His exit was a different matter. He left in glory, surrounded by friends.

✳

Track and field has a running event called a relay. A sprinter races to his teammate and hands off a baton. The phrase "passing the baton" comes from this event. Forty days after his resurrection, Jesus led his disciples to Bethany to pass the baton.

The departure may have surprised the disciples, but it shouldn't have. On several occasions Jesus had told them he would ascend into heaven. Still, hearing about it and seeing it were different things.

Jesus first told them their immediate and future tasks (Acts 1:6–11). They were to wait in Jerusalem until the Holy Spirit came upon them, then they were to be his witnesses in Jerusalem, Judea, Samaria, and

Since, then, we have a great high priest who has passed through the heavens, Jesus, the Son of God, let us hold fast to our confession.

Hebrews 4:14 NRSV

Without question, this is the great mystery of our faith: Christ was revealed in a human body and vindicated by the Spirit. He was seen by angels and announced to the nations. He was believed in throughout the world and was taken to heaven in glory.

1 Timothy 3:16 NLT

"the remotest part of the earth" (v. 8 NASB). This was a very organized command. The disciples were to tell the message of Jesus first in the city of Jerusalem, then in the region of Judea, then farther out to Samaria, and finally into the whole known earth. If this had happened in the United States, Jesus might have told his disciples to be witnesses in Los Angeles, California, the entire United States, and the rest of the world. Jesus passed the baton.

Luke revealed that Jesus raised his hands and blessed them, and while he was doing so he was "carried up into heaven" (Luke 24:51 NKJV). In the middle of blessing his disciples, his hands raised, Jesus ascended. They watched him go until he disappeared into a cloud.

Final Thought

The ascension is more than a dramatic exit; it's a reminder that Jesus was returning to his place in heaven, the place he left to come to earth. It was not an end of Jesus' work, but the beginning of the church's work—a work that continues to this day.

Check Your Understanding

- **The ascension is tied to a future event involving Jesus that has fascinating parallels. What future event might that be?**

The second coming of Jesus. Jesus ascended physically and will return physically. He rose into the sky; he will return from the sky. He disappeared into a cloud; he will appear again from a cloud (Acts 1:11).

- **What do you suppose the disciples' response was to seeing Jesus ascend into the air?**

At first they were stunned and "two men in white clothing" (angels) had to prompt them to bring their attention earthward again (Acts 1:10–11 NASB). They were also filled with worship and great joy (Luke 24:52–53).

How Jesus Changed the World

The work of Jesus didn't end two thousand years ago; it was just beginning. Jesus' impact on the world is clearly seen everywhere. Much is owed to those who took his message to the world.

Contents

He commanded us to preach to the people and to testify
that he is the one whom God appointed as judge
of the living and the dead.

Acts 10:42 NIV

Working Through the Apostles

The United States has a little more than 130 ambassadors scattered around the world representing the U.S. government and people to countries from Afghanistan to Zimbabwe. Current events change the number of ambassadors in the field, but the mission remains the same: to speak on behalf of the country and its leaders. An ambassador is an appointed individual who represents one country on the soil of another. An apostle is very much the same thing, except he represents Jesus to the world. A handful of men would take over where Jesus left off, just as Jesus commanded them to do.

After Judas's betrayal of Jesus and his subsequent suicide, eleven men were left to carry out the mission of Jesus. There were 120 or so other disciples, but the eleven were the first to bear the title *apostle*. They had gone through a roller coaster of emotions, from the joy and satisfaction of traveling with Jesus to the ultimate despair that came with seeing him die on the cross. The resurrection enlivened them again, but they were still too meek to do all Jesus had called them to do. Before his ascension, he commissioned them to start in Jerusalem and then go into the world.

First, they were to wait in Jerusalem for the promised outpouring of the Holy Spirit. The second chapter of Acts describes that event. The sudden, empowering arrival of the Holy Spirit changed the men. They

I never shrank back from telling you what you needed to hear, either publicly or in your homes. I have had one message for Jews and Greeks alike—the necessity of repenting from sin and turning to God, and of having faith in our Lord Jesus.

Acts 20:20–21 NLT

Peter told them many other things as well. Then he said, "I beg you to save yourselves from what will happen to all these evil people." On that day about three thousand believed his message and were baptized.

Acts 2:40–41 CEV

preached and taught wherever they went. This took great courage because the people who had Jesus killed were still around. Yet the fear of death didn't slow them at all. Peter took the lead. Before long thousands joined the church and Peter was routinely arrested. Paul, who persecuted the church only to later become an apostle, was accused of "turning the world upside down" (Acts 17:6 NRSV).

The apostles moved out from Jerusalem and into the world. History lost track of most of them, but the results of their efforts have changed the world forever. The men that Jesus changed—fishermen, a tax collector, and others—were changed into men who truly turned the world upside down.

Final Thought

Some argue that Christianity is the creation of a few bent on misleading others. The Bible lists some who died for the faith, and tradition states that every apostle but one was martyred in ways that included death by crucifixion, beheading, flaying, stoning, and beatings. They died for something they knew to be true.

Check Your Understanding

- **What made the difference in the lives of the apostles? What could change men so much that they could affect the world so with their preaching and teaching?**

Empowered spiritually by God, motivated by love, prepared by all they had experienced with Jesus, energized by the resurrection, and obedient to the command of Jesus, the apostles became changed men who changed the world.

- **What made their preaching so effective?**

Preaching was effective because of personal experience and the work of the Holy Spirit. Each man had been profoundly changed by Jesus, and they knew the gospel would change countless others.

Working Through the Church

The church is ubiquitous. A world traveler could attend a church service in a different country every week, from Moscow to Johannesburg to Singapore to Washington DC. Major cities and tiny towns have churches. Still, most people misunderstand what a church is. When a person hears the word *church,* he or she is likely to conjure up an image of a building. The church has nothing to do with buildings, and it has everything to do with people.

✳

It is interesting to note that as often as we use the word *church,* Jesus used it only twice during his earthly ministry, and those events are recorded only by Matthew (Jesus used the term quite a few times in the book of Revelation).

The word, which appears 112 times in the New Testament, translates a Greek word that means "assembly," and that gives us our first clue about what the church is and how Jesus used it.

The church is not a building. People tend to make shorthand of complicated ideas or complex statements. Instead of saying, "I'm going to the church building on the corner," we say, "I'm going to church on the corner." The church is made up of people, not brick and mortar. If a church building is destroyed by flood or fire, the church remains intact—only the building is gone.

He is the head of the body, the church, who is the beginning, the first-born from the dead, that in all things He may have the preeminence.

Colossians 1:18 NKJV

I rejoice in my sufferings for your sake, and in my flesh I do my share on behalf of His body, which is the church, in filling up what is lacking in Christ's afflictions.

Colossians 1:24 NASB

The church is made up of the living and the dead. Theologians divide the church into two groups: local and universal. The local church is composed of believers who gather to worship, pray, minister, learn, and support one another. Usually they do this in a building they own or rent. Some churches meet in homes. Church buildings come in all sizes. Churches have started in chicken coops, storefronts, garages. Some church buildings can hold tens of thousands of people. Whatever the size, the church is made not by the building, but by the people who hold a common belief in Jesus.

The universal church consists of all the believers through the ages. Death doesn't remove someone from the universal church. Today's church people belong to the same church as Peter, James, John, and others from centuries before. The New Testament uses several metaphors to describe this church. First is the "body of Christ." The apostle Paul put it this way: "He put all things under His feet, and gave Him to be head over all things to the church, which is His body, the fullness of Him who fills all in all" (Ephesians 1:22–23 NKJV). The metaphor teaches that Jesus is the sole founder and source for the church. He is and forever will be the head of the church.

The New Testament sometimes refers to the church as the bride of Christ (2 Corinthians 11:2). Weddings and marriage were important events to the ancient Jews. The concept shows Jesus' love for the church (its people) is like what a groom feels for his bride. Jesus' love for the church also reveals his lifelong commitment to the church.

Another metaphor for the church is a temple (1 Peter 2:4–8), where people make up the stones and structure and Jesus is the cornerstone. A cornerstone was a large flat stone set in the ground that served as the starting point for the rest of the building. Jesus is the foundation of the church, and the people make up the rest of the building.

These three primary illustrations of the church show the unbreakable bond between Jesus and his church. He is as connected to the church as a head is connected to the body, as a groom is to his bride, as a foundation is to the building it supports. When people become part of the church, they become connected to Jesus.

The church came into being through Jesus' death. Paul put it this way: "Husbands, love your wives, just as Christ also loved the church and gave Himself for her, that He might sanctify and cleanse her with the washing of water by the word, that He might present her to Himself a glorious church, not having spot or wrinkle or any such thing, but that she should be holy and without blemish" (Ephesians 5:25–27 NKJV). The church didn't spring up as a nonprofit organization, but as a vital, powerful force in the world, an organization for which Jesus died.

> Paul, a prisoner of Christ Jesus, and Timothy our brother, to Philemon our dear friend and co-worker, to Apphia our sister, to Archippus our fellow soldier, and to the church in your house: Grace to you and peace from God our Father and the Lord Jesus Christ.
>
> Philemon 1–3 NRSV

Myth Buster

Jesus founded only one institution. He did not start schools, colleges, governments, or any other organization. He started the church to change people and to change the world. The history of organized religion is spotty, tainted by abuses in some cases and by sacrificial works in others. Some argue the church is unneeded. "I love Jesus," they say, "but not the church."

This is similar to saying, "I love to play football, but I don't want to join a team." The Christian belongs in a vital, vibrate, local church. To turn one's back on the church is to diminish the organization Jesus considered his bride.

Final Thought

 The church has one purpose, to draw attention to God through Jesus and to help Christians help one another. There are many denominations, but only one church. Nowhere in the New Testament do we see a Christian apart from a church. The two go together.

Check Your Understanding

- **Why do you suppose so many people avoid church?**

There are probably as many reasons as there are people, but many avoid attending church because they find it boring or irrelevant. There are certainly local churches that fit that description, but there are so many local churches to choose from that the excuse loses credibility. Every Christian belongs in a church.

- **How can a Christian make church more meaningful?**

The mistake that many make is expecting someone else to take responsibility for how interesting a church service is. By remembering how the church came to be in the first place will raise the importance of attending. Usually people get out of church what they put in.

- **Are there hypocrites in church?**

There are hypocrites everywhere: church, home, business, government, hospitals—everywhere. The church is not a collection of perfect people; it's a collection of imperfect people trying to be better.

The Persecutor Who Met Jesus

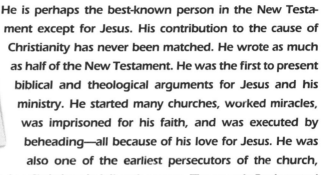

He is perhaps the best-known person in the New Testament except for Jesus. His contribution to the cause of Christianity has never been matched. He wrote as much as half of the New Testament. He was the first to present biblical and theological arguments for Jesus and his ministry. He started many churches, worked miracles, was imprisoned for his faith, and was executed by beheading—all because of his love for Jesus. He was also one of the earliest persecutors of the church, leaving Christians in jail or the grave. The apostle Paul started as the church's greatest enemy and then became its greatest proponent.

✳

Paul seemed the least likely person to spread the gospel around the known world. His given name was Saul, and he was a rising star in the religious community. A Jew by birth, a Pharisee by choice, he had charted a path to the top ranks of the religious leaders. Although we have no physical description of him, tradition describes him as small and unattractive. What he lacked in physical appeal, he made up for in zeal. Saul was a mover and a shaker.

Saul hated Christians, but it wasn't the kind of hate that led to name-calling. That wasn't enough. Shortly after the church began to spread, Saul set out to put an end to it. Here's what he said about himself: "I am a Jew, born in Tarsus of Cilicia,

Paul an apostle—sent neither by human commission nor from human authorities, but through Jesus Christ and God the Father, who raised him from the dead—and all the members of God's family who are with me . . .

Galatians 1:1–2 NRSV

Paul dwelt two whole years in his own rented house, and received all who came to him, preaching the kingdom of God and teaching the things which concern the Lord Jesus Christ with all confidence, no one forbidding him.

Acts 28:30–31 NKJV

but brought up in this city, educated under Gamaliel, strictly according to the law of our fathers, being zealous for God just as you all are today. *I persecuted this Way to the death, binding and putting both men and women into prisons,* as also the high priest and all the Council of the elders can testify. From them I also received letters to the brethren, and started off for Damascus in order to bring even those who were there to Jerusalem as prisoners to be punished" (Acts 22:3-5 NASB, emphasis added). "The Way" was what the early church called itself.

How does such a man become an apostle who sacrificed himself in service to Jesus? The New Testament lists twelve postresurrection appearances of Jesus. The twelfth was to Saul as he traveled to Damascus to persecute more Christians. His encounter was unpleasant. A bright light appeared, and Paul was knocked to the ground. The book of Acts

describes it this way: "As he was traveling, it happened that he was approaching Damascus, and suddenly a light from heaven flashed around him; and he fell to the ground and heard a voice saying to him, 'Saul, Saul, why are you persecuting Me?' And he said, 'Who are You, Lord?' And He said, 'I am Jesus whom you are persecuting, but get up and enter the city, and it will be told you what you must do'" (Acts 9:3-6 NASB). The encounter left Paul blind. It was a harsh conversion experience. Paul would be healed of his blindness and a few years later become the great missionary he is remembered as today.

The apostle took three missionary journeys, traveling far from home and enduring hardships. He listed some of the things he faced in a letter to the church at Corinth: "Beaten times without number, often in danger of death. Five times I received from the Jews thirty-nine lashes. Three times I was beaten with rods, once I was stoned, three times I was shipwrecked, a night and a day I have spent in the deep. I have been on frequent journeys, in dangers from rivers, dangers from robbers, dangers from my countrymen, dangers from the Gentiles, dangers in the city, dangers in the wilderness, dangers on the sea, dangers among false brethren; I have been in labor and hardship, through many sleepless nights, in hunger and thirst, often without food, in cold and exposure. Apart from such external things, there is the daily pressure on me of concern for all the churches" (2 Corinthians 11:23–28 NASB). This he endured because of his love for Jesus, whom he once persecuted.

> I, Paul, write this greeting in my own hand. Remember my chains. Grace be with you.
>
> Colossians 4:18 NIV

Paul was a writer. Of the twenty-seven books in the New Testament, Paul wrote half of them. His writing continued to educate people about what it means to be a Christian. Paul wrote with an honesty seldom seen, at times asserting his authority while a short time later admitting his faults. In each of his letters (some of which he wrote while in prison), he defended the faith, encouraged the faithful, challenged false teachers, and revealed his love for Jesus.

Myth Buster

Some people believe that Jesus is just for the weak-minded. Nothing could be further from the truth. Throughout history men and women of keen intellect, quality education, and great skill have professed a belief in Jesus. Scientists, writers, engineers, political leaders, the best from every walk of life have found the claims of Jesus to be true and have invested their belief in him.

Intelligence has never been a hindrance to faith in Jesus. Paul was a true intellectual of his day, and he wasn't afraid to use his intelligence to further the church.

Final Thought

Paul died for his faith. He had endured crushing hardships, but still he continued. Paul had inherited Roman citizenship, which granted him certain privileges. He exercised the privilege to appeal for a hearing before Caesar in Rome. He spent some time under house arrest and was then beheaded.

Check Your Understanding

- **What could change Saul the persecutor of the church into Paul the church starter?**

Clearly, he had a life-changing event. Jesus' appearing to him on the road to Damascus shook Paul to the core. For a time he was blind and helpless. Christians helped him.

- **Why did Saul/Paul persecute the church?**

It sounds odd to say, but he believed he was serving God. To him, Christianity was a cult that threatened Judaism. In his zeal, he felt he was making God happy. In truth, he was doing just the opposite.

- **What role did Paul fill with his ministry?**

After Judas betrayed Jesus, Judas hanged himself. Jesus called twelve disciples to be apostles. Some believe, and rightly so, that Paul replaced Judas in the Twelve.

From Jerusalem to the World the Message Continues

The twenty-first-century mind thinks globally. It's natural and made even more common by television and the Internet. We can place a phone call to anyplace in the world with a cell phone we carry in our pocket. With some money and a passport, a person can fly to any country in the world. One of the largest industries is tourism. Every country wants travelers from other countries to visit and spend money. This was not so in the first century. Short travel was measured in days, long trips in months. Letters were handwritten and hand-carried, and yet the gospel not only spread, it spread quickly.

During years of drought, Australia experiences grass and brush fires. Sometimes these fires spread as fast as a person can run. Those who have seen such fires understand the phrase "It spread like wildfire." In many ways, Christianity spread that quickly. Not just in Jerusalem and the surrounding regions, but in faraway countries. Although they had different names in the first century, countries like Greece, Turkey, Italy, and Egypt had cities with Christian communities. By the end of the second century, churches could be found as far away as Spain and France.

Several things contributed to the church's spread. First was the dedication of men like Paul who

> This gospel of the kingdom shall be preached in the whole world as a testimony to all the nations, and then the end will come.
>
> Matthew 24:14 NASB
>
> Don't forget all the hard times you went through when you first received the light. Sometimes you were abused and mistreated in public, and at other times you shared in the sufferings of others. You were kind to people in jail. And you gladly let your possessions be taken away, because you knew you had something better, something that would last forever.
>
> Hebrews 10:32–34 CEV

endured great hardship to travel to various countries. Paul was a systematic man, often choosing a crossroads city as his focus. Those who embraced the faith took it to their homelands.

As odd as it sounds, persecution also contributed to the church's spread. The early church underwent severe persecution, which often drove Christians from their homes. Some Christians faced economic persecution. In Gentile areas, local guilds had representative Greek or Roman idols. Christians refused to pledge allegiance to any other god, an act that kept them from working their trades. Those disenfranchised believers had to find work elsewhere. Persecution drove Christians out and into the world, and they took their faith with them.

Persecution was like throwing water on an oil fire—it spread the flame. Although persecution was horrible, Christians drew strength from the local churches and the fellowship of other believers. In time, Christianity circled the globe.

Final Thought

 Standing this far removed from the first days of the church makes it difficult to believe that Jesus, by outward appearances a simple carpenter, could start a movement of billions. Anyone in his day would have doubted such a claim, but from the beginning, Jesus said it would happen (Matthew 24:14).

Check Your Understanding

- **Persecution of Christians has not ceased. There are countries where being a Christian remains a life-and-death issue. Why do such people continue in the faith?**

People continue in the faith for the same reason the first-century believers did: their faith is real and is the most valuable thing they possess. For them, hardship is part of the Christian walk.

Personal and Knowable

The resurrection of Jesus messes with time. Physicists talk about time's arrow, the flow of time from the past to the future. We think in those terms. Our speech has three tenses: past, present, and future. Consequently, when we think about Jesus, the tendency is to think about him historically, as if he were confined to those days two thousand years ago. But the whole point of the resurrection was to prove that Jesus continues to live and to change the lives of people.

So what is Jesus doing these days? The disciples thought it all ended with Jesus' death, but he rose again. After forty days of postresurrection appearances, Jesus ascended to heaven. To some that must have appeared to be the final act of the play, but Jesus had given the disciples instructions to take his message to the world. Jesus isn't a historical character who lived and died. He continues to live.

Very soon after the start of the church, a deacon named Stephen saw heaven open and Jesus standing at the right hand of God. The revelation led to his being seized and stoned to death, an illegal act under Roman law. The apostle Paul saw Jesus several times after the ascension (Acts 9:1-9; 1 Corinthians 9:1; 15:9). Only Jesus' physical location has changed. His mission and work continue. What kind of work is Jesus doing now? Certainly, he is doing more than we can imagine, but the Bible lists some of his activities.

> He had to be one of us, so that he could serve God as our merciful and faithful high priest and sacrifice himself for the forgiveness of our sins.
>
> Hebrews 2:17 CEV

> There is one God and one Mediator between God and men, the Man Christ Jesus, who gave Himself a ransom for all, to be testified in due time.
>
> 1 Timothy 2:5–6 NKJV

- *Interceding for his people*. The author of Hebrews (probably Paul) wrote, "He is able to save completely those who come to God through him, because he always lives to intercede for them" (Hebrews 7:25 NIV). Intercession is an act in which one person stands in for another. It is very much like a lawyer who appears in court on behalf of a client. The attorney speaks for and defends his client, even if the client isn't present. John used a different word: "If anyone sins, we have an Advocate with the Father, Jesus Christ the righteous" (1 John 2:1 NASB). Jesus "represents" us before God, providing an unassailable defense.

- *Preparing heaven for us*. In the midst of one of Jesus' promises to return is this interesting statement: "In My Father's house are many mansions; if it were not so, I would have told you. I go to prepare a place for you" (John 14:2 NKJV). Exactly what the preparation entails isn't explained, only that Jesus would go and continue to prepare our place in heaven.

- *Building his church*. At one point in his ministry, Jesus asked his disciples who people said he was. They gave several answers, 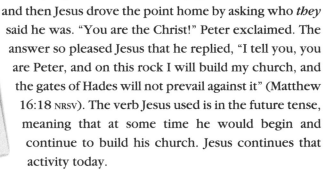 and then Jesus drove the point home by asking who *they* said he was. "You are the Christ!" Peter exclaimed. The answer so pleased Jesus that he replied, "I tell you, you are Peter, and on this rock I will build my church, and the gates of Hades will not prevail against it" (Matthew 16:18 NRSV). The verb Jesus used is in the future tense, meaning that at some time he would begin and continue to build his church. Jesus continues that activity today.

- *Indwelling the believer*. Indwelling refers to the act of living in something. We indwell our houses or apartments. Jesus indwells his followers, spiritually taking up residence. Paul said it this way: "It is no longer I who live, but Christ lives in me. So I live in this earthly body by trusting in the Son of God, who loved me and gave himself for me" (Galatians 2:20 NLT).

- *Being High Priest*. In ancient Judaism, the high priest served several functions, the greatest of which was making the sacrifice for the sins of the people. This he did on the Day of Atonement, a special day, by entering the Holy of Holies. Jesus became the High Priest and made the sacrifice for sin with his own life. "We do not have a high priest who is unable to sympathize with our weaknesses, but we have one who has been tempted in every way, just as we are—yet was without sin. Let us then approach the throne of grace with confidence, so that we may receive mercy and find grace to help us in our time of need" (Hebrews 4:15-16 NIV).

To them God chose to make known how great among the Gentiles are the riches of the glory of this mystery, which is Christ in you, the hope of glory.

Colossians 1:27 NRSV

Digging Deeper

There's a myth that Jesus is a past-tense Savior and that his day ended two thousand years ago. Christians through the ages have thought otherwise. They have lived their lives with a solid belief that Jesus is as much alive and as active as ever before. The biblical testimony is that he works now and will continue to do his work for eternity. At some point Jesus will come again, but not even that ends his activity. Not only does Jesus live, but his ministry also lives among his people.

Final Thought

 It has often been said that religion is humankind reaching for God; Christianity is God reaching for humankind. Having a living Savior makes Christianity unique. Out of sight doesn't mean out of mind.

Check Your Understanding

- Is it difficult to believe that Jesus continues his work two thousand years later?

It is for some, and that's understandable. It goes against normal experience. People are born, and they live, and then they die, and that never changes. Jesus is the exception. He did live and die, but continues to live today. The ascension did not end Jesus' ministry.

- What does it say about Jesus that he has continued his work over the centuries?

It says that his focus on humanity has not wavered, that more work needs to be done, and that there are still many lives that need to be changed.

- What does it mean to you that Jesus continues his work?

It means that you can have a relationship with a living Savior, not a past-tense one; that Jesus' love can't be altered by the passing of years.

Peace be to the brethren, and love with faith, from God the Father and the Lord Jesus Christ. Grace be with all those who love our Lord Jesus Christ with incorruptible love.

Ephesians 6:23–24 NASB

Jesus Christ turns life right-side-up, and heaven outside-in.

Carl F. Henry

May the grace of the Lord Jesus Christ, and the love of God,
and the fellowship of the Holy Spirit be with you all.

2 Corinthians 13:14 NIV

Grace, mercy and peace will be with us, from God the Father and from Jesus Christ, the Son of the Father, in truth and love.

2 John 3 NASB

Books in The Indispensable Guide to Practically Everything
series include:

The Indispensable Guide to Practically Everything:
The Bible

The Indispensable Guide to Practically Everything:
Bible Prophecy and the End Times

The Indispensable Guide to Practically Everything:
Jesus

The Indispensable Guide to Practically Everything:
Life After Death & Heaven and Hell

The Indispensable Guide to Practically Everything:
Prayer

The Indispensable Guide to Practically Everything:
World Religions and What People Believe